MEDIA SKILLS

MAKING A VIDEO

How to produce and present
your own film or programme

Nick Hale

How To Books

Cartoons by Mike Flanagan

British Library Cataloguing in Publication Data
A catalogue record for this book is available from the British Library.

First published in 1997 by How To Books Ltd, 3 Newtec Place,
Magdalen Road, Oxford OX4 1RE, United Kingdom.
Tel: (01865) 793806. Fax: (01865) 248780.

Note: The material contained in this book is set out in good faith for general
guidance and no liability can be accepted for loss or expense incurred as a
result of relying in particular circumstances on statements made in the book.
The laws and regulations are complex and liable to change, and readers
should check the current position with the relevant authorities before making
personal arrangements.

Produced for How To Books by Deer Park Productions.

Typeset by Anneset, Weston super Mare, North Somerset.
Printed and bound by Cromwell Press, Broughton Gifford, Melksham, Wiltshire.

MAKING A VIDEO

Contents

List of Illustrations

Foreword

In virtually the last interview he was ever to give John Grierson told of how, at a conference in Italy, the screenwriter Cesar Zavattini made a witty speech in which he thought it would be wonderful if all the villagers in his homeland were to be armed with cameras so that they could make films by themselves, and in this way write film letters to each other. This was taken as a great joke, and everyone laughed and laughed. Everyone that is except Grierson. 'Because I think that is the next stage.'

Video. That great communicator and founder of the British documentary film saw at once that this was a revolution which would democratise the media. Making it possible for everyone to set up and shoot their own story on the motion picture screen, in their own way, free of outside control or interference. Record an event. Make a statement. Tell a story. Package a show. Launch a crusade . . . Individual or Group.

So go ahead, and make it happen yourself. But always remember that if there is more to the making of a film than sitting in a folding chair and calling 'Action', then there is none the less also a great deal more to making a successful and effective video programme than just pointing the camera and pressing the button. In the pages that follow I am happy to welcome the most detailed, informative, and experienced step by step signposting that has yet to come my way.

Peter Hopkinson

Preface

Many of us have had the thought at one time or another, 'Couldn't we make a video about it?' Perhaps we think, 'Oh, but that's for the professionals and it's all much too expensive' or 'Amateur videos are just for family and friends.'

There was a time when films were made by professionals working in the film industry (which is still alive and kicking), making feature films, documentaries, and sponsored films. Then came television, making programmes, some factual, some fiction, using electronic as well as film cameras. Most recently the domestic camcorder arrived. Now, in theory, anyone can make a video. The technology has become more accessible, but at the same time the choices have become more bewildering. And with audiences becoming more visually sophisticated, the business of effective communication with images and sound is no less complex than before.

So now the gap between professional and amateur needs to be filled. Perhaps it is possible to make that video after all. Maybe the money can be found. This book aims to introduce you to the process, guiding you from conception through production to final delivery and exhibition. The more you know about it the more likely you are to succeed not only in surmounting the pitfalls and obstacles, but also in coming up with something a bit above the average.

One can't write a book like this entirely on one's own, and I would like to thank Robert Angell, Frances Berrigan, Roland Brinton, Charles Frater, James Harpham and Michael Rabiger for their help, advice and inspiration, and Catherine for her wordprocessing skills. I of course remain responsible for what is said, and I hope that it will inspire you, the reader, to have a go.

Nick Hale

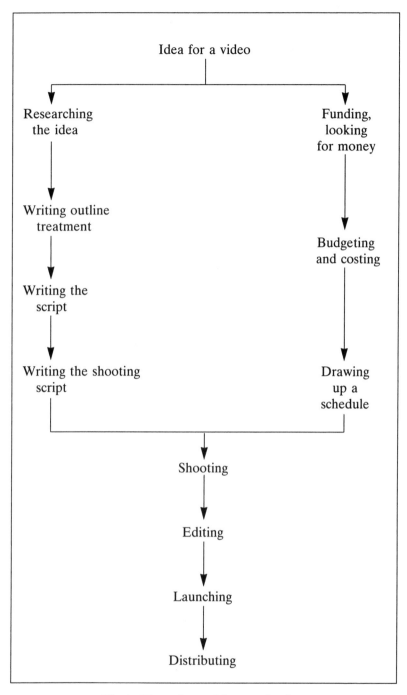

Fig 1. Flow chart: video production

1
Exploring the Possibilities

INTRODUCTION

The optically recorded image has been around since the invention of photography, early in the last century. It was, and still is, put to all sorts of uses. Then came the moving image, and later, in the middle of this century, came television with the possibilities of electronically distributing moving images with sound. Now, with the development of the video camcorder and player, you have the possibility of electronically recording and distributing images with sound – in other words, making a video.

POSSIBLE FIELDS

Corporate
There are all sorts of uses for video within a corporation or institution. Employer training and induction, company reports, company history, company news and, of course, selling the product.

Teaching
Anyone involved in education knows the importance of arousing the students' interest and enthusiasm for a subject. Video is an ideal way to encourage further study.

Community history
Most communities have a lot of buried treasure. People have collections of old photographs in the attic, and senior citizens are generally only too pleased to record their memories of times past.

Journalism
There are many instances where images can reveal much more of what is going on in a newsworthy situation than a newspaper or radio account.

Fundraising
A video to show to potential donors can illustrate very graphically not only the problem that needs to be tackled, but also the results of a charity's works.

Recording expeditions
As well as being a souvenir for those on the trip, a video record of an exciting venture could have a wider appeal, or even an instructional element for others considering a similar venture.

Counselling
A video can be used to give clients a general background to the topic, helping to make them feel less isolated, or it could serve to train other counsellors.

Evangelising
Of course, trying to convert the world by distributing a video is a tall order, but on a more practical level it's an ideal way for bishops to address their flocks in distant parts.

Choreography,
Video is invaluable as an archival record of a performance, capturing the spirit as well as the steps. Nor need it just sit in an archive – it can be used to promote the choreographer's work. Some choreographers even create specifically for the camera.

Weddings
Moving pictures with sound is bound to be an improvement over the wedding photograph, and copies can be sent to absent friends and relatives. The same applies to other events such as births, christenings, funerals, family reunions, graduation balls, etc.

Anthropology
Video provides an invaluable method of recording data on unique events or customs in closed communities. The material can then be analysed later at leisure, and could be edited into a visual treatise.

Curriculum vitae
Make your CV on video. It could be cheaper to send a video to present yourself than to book a day return on Concorde for a job interview in New York.

Music
The music industry is always hungry for videos, whether to promote an up and coming group or to launch a new album.

Politics
Politicians are campaigners, and if they can get access to television to reach a wider audience, they can construct their own message with a video rather than just being interviewed by the TV station.

Medicine
Procedures for new operating techniques can best be illustrated for others by making a video.

Cooking
Recipes for exotic dishes are all very well for those who are already expert cooks, but for most of us there is no substitute for actually seeing it being made. Witness the popularity of cooking programmes on television.

Communicating with images
Of course, the above list is not meant to be comprehensive. Whatever field you work in or interests you have, you could find yourself in the position of needing to make a video, either at your own or at someone else's instigation. You may say, 'Well, I'm much too busy doing my thing to get involved in making videos.' But perhaps you could delegate it to a colleague or employee.

You don't have to be a professional media person to make a successful video, any more than you have to be a professional author to write a book. If you have got something to say and you think there is an audience, then this book will help you become familiar with the process of making a video. Most of us are as literate visually as we are verbally, some of us more so, and there is really no more mystique about communication with images than there is about writing words.

DIVIDING UP THE WORK

Perhaps you have been asked to make a video, and implicit in that request is that you will be liaising with the person who delegated the task to you. Now you, in turn, have to decide what functions, if any, you are going to delegate.

If you look at the chapter headings of this book you will see that there are quite a number of processes and procedures involved in making a video:

- research
- scripting
- budgeting
- scheduling
- shooting
- editing
- presenting

to name but a few. If you decide not to delegate, and do virtually everything yourself, then you will be in danger of contracting what (with apologies to the medical profession) might be called 'multiple schizophrenia'. You will split into not just two different personalities but quite a few others as well, like photographer, researcher, recordist, editor, production manager, and last but not least, cost cutter. Each of these selves within you will have differing needs and ambitions and there will be potential for a lot of conflict – hence the disease of schizophrenia.

For example, the photographer in you wants to shoot the chairman's speech in the middle of a funfair, but the sound recordist in you points out that you won't hear a word he says. Here we have conflicting aims, and someone – you – has to find a solution.

Adjudicating and monitoring

You have to be an adjudicator, and it will almost certainly be easier on you if you adjudicate between real people in the real world rather than conflicting parts of your own self.

Depending on the size and complexity of your video project, you will need some help, but, as always when delegating a function, it's a good idea to know something about that function yourself. That way you can monitor the performance of the person you have chosen, and they will feel they can communicate their concerns to someone who understands the problem.

POSSIBLE ROUTES

On the following page are several approaches you could adopt in order to make a video. Which is the most appropriate will depend on how much time you have, how much money you can get hold of and how complex your project is.

1. *DIY (Do It Yourself)*, maybe with friends. Suitable for low-budget, non-broadcast projects where there is plenty of time. Risk of schizophrenia, as outlined above.

2. *Using 'in-house' facilities*. You may have access to corporate or institutional video facilities. This may involve scheduling your project in with other projects, which could be a constraint. On the other hand, you probably get technical help along with the equipment.

3. *Approaching a professional production company*. This will cost money. However, they will be able to provide all the facilities and help that you need, including producing and directing. If your idea is accepted by a commissioning editor, in one of the broadcast television companies, for instance, you will almost certainly be steered towards a particular production company known to the commissioning editor. You can find lists of production companies in trade journals and production manuals, with an indication of the kind of projects they specialise in. (See the Useful Addresses section at the back of this book.)

4. *Using 'workshop' facilities*. These are usually non-profitmaking organisations, often grant aided, which are set up specifically to enable film or video projects to be undertaken at minimum cost. They offer equipment for shooting and editing at subsidised rates, though it's unlikely to be the most up-to-date equipment. Some even run courses on how to use the equipment. There is a list of these in the United Kingdom in the Useful Addresses section.

A combination of DIY and workshops may be the answer if your funds are limited but you have the necessary perseverance.

The later chapters in this book will outline the main functions and procedures involved in making a video, and the Further Reading section at the end will suggest some more specialised areas of study. But before immersing yourself in procedures, it is as well first to consider just who will want to see your video.

2
Targeting your Audience

SPECIFYING THE VIEWER

If you have a video project in mind, you will most probably have an audience in mind as well. Indeed it may well be your special knowledge of the needs of a group of people which has prompted you to think about making a video. Consider the following groups:

- athletes
- the bereaved
- colleagues
- doctors
- employees
- employers
- friends and relatives
- house-buyers
- housewives
- politicians
- the public, who watch TV
- the public with money to give
- the public with money to spend
- students
- tourists
- voters

Now consider the 'possible fields' listed in Chapter 1. They are linked, but do not necessarily coincide exactly. For any given field, or subject matter, there may be more than one potential audience. Which is *your* audience is an important question. You will need to identify exactly who you are aiming at if you are to avoid making a diffuse 'catch-all' video which doesn't really hit home with anybody.

DEFINING THE SCOPE

How much should you try to include in your video project? Here are three examples of subject matter, taken from actual projects, to show how the scope of your video is dependent on the audience.

1. *Water shortage.* A civil servant in a Middle Eastern country commissions a video about an acute problem of water supply and pollution, to be shown only to the Sultan and his cabinet. It is a problem which requires an urgent solution, and which they can all be made aware of at one showing more effectively than by distributing written reports to each individual. It is made for a small audience for a specific purpose, and will be very different from a video which was made to be shown on national television as an appeal to the population to use water sparingly.

2. *Autism.* A video might be made at regular intervals over a period of time to assess whether there is any discernible improvement in a group of children being treated for autism. Such a video will be aimed at specialists in the field of autism, and will be very different from a documentary made to enlighten parents about the problem of autistic children.

3. *Rural technology.* A video about a new economical wood-burning stove designed to be used in rural Africa might be aimed at those who are to make and use it, or it might be aimed at audiences in developed countries who might donate money for the project. The same video would not do for both audiences.

It is important to be clear in your mind, and to make it clear to collaborators, exactly who your audience is and what the scope of the video will be before you can write an effective script, which will be the next task.

Identifying your audience will help you define more precisely the scope of your video.

3
Writing the Script

INTRODUCTION

Literature has the problem of making the significant somehow visible, while film often finds itself trying to make the visible significant. (Richardson, *Literature and the Film*, Indiana University Press 1969)

The script is not a piece of literature. You could say that it is a way of indicating how the visible will be significant. It is not 'the book of the film', but a working blueprint of a finished video, in the same way that an architect's drawing is not a building but will nevertheless tell someone else what that building will look like.

Your completed video will be viewed in a matter of ten minutes, or half an hour, depending on its length. The viewer will see it as a total experience, all in one go, without flipping backwards and forwards as one might in a book. You need to bear this in mind when writing your script. Your idea, or message, must unfold clearly step by step for the viewer. This does not mean that you cannot juggle with time, simply that the viewer has no opportunity to sort out any confusion by referring back.

DEFINING THE PURPOSE

Before you sit down and face your blank sheet of paper, ask yourself what your video will be doing. Will it be:

- selling
- persuading
- informing
- educating
- entertaining
- preaching
- investigating

- expressing an opinion
- documenting
- reporting
- training
- recruiting
- fundraising
- campaigning
- counselling?

It could be doing more than one of these. You might even say that in most cases, entertaining is the single most important purpose. If your audience is bored then you will fail to inform, sell, educate, counsel, train or whatever. The fact that your video may be doing more than one thing does not necessarily mean that it will be more diffuse and therefore less effective, so long as you keep in mind the needs of your audience.

Consider the following examples:

1. *A straightforward wedding video*. You will be documenting, perhaps reporting, and certainly entertaining. Intended audience? Friends and relatives of the happy couple. Its purpose will be to serve as a memento of a happy occasion.

2. *A video on bereavement*. You will certainly be counselling, perhaps informing, or reporting, or even investigating. You will need to ask yourself whether you are addressing those who are suffering bereavement (counselling), or those who are helping the bereaved (training), or those who are simply anxious to know what to expect when bereavement occurs (informing). If you were counselling the bereaved you would need to be tactful and circumspect to avoid upsetting or angering the sufferers, whereas if you are dealing with the subject as a social phenomenon, you can perhaps afford to be more direct in portraying how death and loss are coped with.

3. *A sales video*. Suppose you make caravans, and you want to sell more caravans. You could make a video which showed the advantages and superiority of your caravans over other makes, or you could make a video showing the advantages and possibilities of taking a holiday with a caravan rather than staying in hotels, hoping that converts will buy your make rather than another. The first would be selling and persuading, aimed at people who already want to buy a caravan. The second would be informing, persuading and soft selling, aimed at people who want to go on holiday.

It is tempting to try and kill as many birds as possible with one stone, either for financial reasons, to save having to make more than one video, or for egotistical reasons, like establishing a claim to have made the definitive video on a subject. This temptation needs to be resisted, otherwise your video will be less effective.

> Being clear about the purpose of your video will help define who your audience is going to be.

RESEARCHING AND PREPARING

For any but the most straightforward projects you will need to do some research, particularly if the task of making the video has been delegated to you. You may even decide it is worthwhile to bring in a researcher to do it for you. Nevertheless, he or she will need to be briefed by you.

Researching the subject

This is likely to involve:

- visiting libraries to get background material from books

- writing letters to people whom you think might have something to contribute or opinions to express

- contacting government departments or large corporations for statistical information

- finding out what other videos may have already been made in your field, and viewing them

- visiting picture libraries for archive material, both still and moving.

All sorts of ideas for enhancing the interest of your video, or fresh angles on the subject, will occur to you as you are researching. Note them all down at the time in some sort of diary. Later you can sort through it all and decide what is actually going to be relevant to your purpose. In any case, the wider your knowledge of the subject the more impressive you will seem to collaborators or possible sponsors.

Researching the market

It may be worthwhile to verify that there really is an audience out there for your video. Carry out your own market research.

- How many people are likely to want to see it?

- What viewing facilities are they likely to have?

- Will they be willing to pay and if so, how much?

- Are there likely to be audiences in foreign countries who would need a version in their own language?

The answers to these questions may affect the amount of money that will be needed to finance the video and will also give an indication of what might have to be done to distribute it, or enable it to be seen.

Example: African wood-burning stove
Take the third example in Chapter 2 about the wood-burning stove to be used in rural Africa. If the video is aimed at those who will make and use it, they are unlikely to have domestic VCRs (video cassette recorders) for viewing, so arrangements would have to be made for group viewing in villages if such facilities don't already exist. There may be several different languages spoken, even over a quite small geographical area, so you might have to make several versions, which would increase your costs.

If the video is aimed at audiences in developed countries, to raise funds, it would be better to aim at group viewings where there is a captive audience, in church halls or charitable society meetings, rather that rely on home viewing, which would involve a large number of copies.

Consulting with colleagues

Most video projects will involve other people who will want to be consulted. Even with a wedding video you will need to consult the future in-laws as well as your own family.

In a corporate or institutional environment there will be people in other departments who may have an interest in your project, and whose co-operation you will need later in shooting the video. They may also have suggestions about what should be included in the video, and this is where you will have to play the role of diplomat.

They may be helping you to define the purpose of your video, or they may be trying to add on other interests which, while valid in themselves, would only diffuse the impact of your video. So if the purpose of your video is already defined, you will have to be tactful in explaining it to them and explaining why their co-operation will be needed.

Example: selling caravans
Take the third example in this chapter of a company that wants to sell caravans. You have decided to try and sell the idea of caravanning rather than staying in hotels. The research and development department are keen to include a sequence showing the manufacture of the new suspension system they have spent so much time and effort in developing. You feel that this would be likely to bore an audience whom you are trying to wean onto caravans, even though it would be appropriate if you were making the other video about the advantages and superiority of your caravans over other makes.

A decision has to be made, and it is better to make it early on in the research and consultation stage, rather than after the video has been shot.

Selecting participants

Whether you are going to interview people, or have them speak directly to the camera, or ask them to behave as they normally would in their job or function, you will need to ask yourself:

- Are they articulate and concise?

- Are they co-operative?

- Do they know their subject?

- Are they likely to be prima donnas?

- Will they be available when you want them?

This kind of research can take up a lot of time, but it will be time well spent. When selecting interviewees you should take an audio tape recorder with you, but explain to them that you are using it only as a form of note taking. Even if you decide not to use that person, or they decide they don't want to participate, you may still glean useful information or opinions from them. You can also form some idea from the audio tape as to how they come across, and how articulate they are.

A further advantage is that it may encourage the person to reformulate their ideas more concisely during the time between your initial meeting with them and the subsequent interview on camera.

> Time spent consulting colleagues, thinking through the scope and implications of your subject, and vetting participants, will never be wasted. Once you start shooting it will be too late to do the groundwork.

PUTTING PEN TO PAPER

Blocking out
You have a blank sheet of paper in front of you. How do you write down the script? The answer is that you will have already started writing the script with your research notes, and even earlier when you defined the purpose of your video.

The simplest procedure is to start by setting out the aim of your video and listing the main points to be covered. You will probably do this for your own benefit as well as the benefit of colleagues during the early stages of your research.

Storytelling
A question which you should ask yourself is, 'Is there a story to be told?' A story may be what started you off on the idea of making a video in the first place. Or it may be something you can impose on the subject. Most audiences, even specialist ones, like a story.

Who will tell the story? It could be the participants among themselves (as in a drama video), or the participants could address you, or the camera, or you could tell the story in the form of narration with pictures.

Example: holiday video
A father wants to make a video of the family holiday. Most people get no further than getting out the camcorder at odd moments to film a visit, or a swim in the sea, and the result, while it may bring back memories for the family in the future, will probably bore anyone else. But if Dad gets Mum and the kids to explain to the camera what they are doing and where they want to go and why, maybe with a little prompting from Dad, then personalities, as well as places, are portrayed and something more like a story develops.

There is no reason why such techniques cannot be used with more 'serious' subjects. It may be possible to devise a story line, with a beginning, a middle and an end, which will incorporate your list of points to be covered.

Using dreams

There are occasions when the brief may require you to deliver a tactful lesson to your audience.

Example: safety video
You work in a company whose employees are asked to undertake dangerous procedures, and there have been instances where safety procedures have been neglected by department managers. You have been asked to make a video to be shown to managers in order to drive home the necessity of correct observance of safety procedures. Rather than simply writing up a story showing the horrendous consequences of not following correct procedure, which might alienate some managers who feel themselves to be above criticism, you could incorporate the story into a dream sequence. Everyone can identify with a character who has dreams without feeling they are being criticised directly.

Presenting the idea

Having thought about

- the purpose
- the intended audience
- whose views are going to be expressed
- the narrative possibilities
- all the points you need to cover

you are now in a position to write an outline treatment which will probably be no more than one side of A4 paper. It will be a skeleton treatment which will make it clear to anyone else what the video will cover and what its purpose is. Your colleagues can read it and make further suggestions or comments, or you can send it to commissioning editors to see if the subject interests them. If it does, they will probably ask you to develop the idea further, and to submit a more detailed treatment.

An outline treatment (see the example in Figure 2) will cover:

- the intention
- the method
- the approach
- the ground to be covered.

Bereavement Foundation Ltd   reg. charity no 54321
7 Somewhere St
Big City

Proposed 20 min video
Working title 'Help for the Bereaved'

Aim: To help recently bereaved people to accept their loss, and to adjust their lives to new circumstances.

Intended audience: Those who have recently lost their spouse, parent, child or other close relative or friend.

The Reverend Wellbeloved, an expert on bereavement, will introduce the video, and emphasise the importance of grieving, and of allowing the emotions an outlet. A selection of people who suffered bereavement in the past will be interviewed, ranging from those who are relatively stoical to the more seemingly distressed, to illustrate how people differ in their reactions to bereavement. Those selected for interview will include people who have lost children or parents, as well as spouses.

The interviews will be interspersed with sequences showing various funeral procedures and the varying types of mementoes used to commemorate the dead, in particular showing old photographs of grandparents and ancestors, in order to emphasise the continuity of life from generation to generation. Some of the interview voices will be laid over these images.

If possible, examples from different cultural and religious backgrounds found in the United Kingdom will be included, but the commentary will be deliberately non-specific about religious beliefs.

Finally, the Reverend Wellbeloved will summarise the points made by the interviewees, and suggest ways in which the viewer could seek further help.

Fig. 2. Sample outline treatment.

Fleshing it out

This is where you put the flesh onto the skeleton outline treatment. Commentary and music will be indicated. Interviewees will be listed and identified and the likely content of their interviews will be summarised. Visual sequences and their intended mood will be elaborated, and the probable order of sequences will be worked out. The purpose of the video and its intended effect on the audience may also be more fully spelled out.

The result should be a layman's blueprint as to what the video will look and sound like. You can circulate it to colleagues and prospective participants, submit it to commissioning editors, or use it to raise funds for the project.

Remembering the key points

1. Your outline treatment will emerge as you do your initial research.

2. Your full treatment will be the result of further research, including audio interviews, permissions to film, and selection of participants.

3. You should assume that your video will be viewed as a one-off experience. Does your treatment take this into account?

DEVISING A PLAN

Once you start shooting you will need a plan in order to keep your head above water. This means having a **shooting script** – yet another sort of script! It is what you will use in your role as director.

Your shooting script

There are at least two reasons for having a shooting script, apart from being an aide-memoire when shooting.

1. It compels you to think out in advance and in detail how each scene and shot will work, and what the commentary will be saying at that point.

2. It enables you or your production manager to work out a detailed schedule and budget for shooting.

If you have seen or read shooting scripts for feature films, known as screenplays, you may be tempted to let your imagination run, and start straight in on a shooting script for your project. It would be unlikely to bear much relation to the reality of the shooting situation. A successful shooting script will be the result of your painstaking research, and your visits to possible shooting locations.

Of course, some subjects are by their nature unpredictable in the sense that you cannot write out in advance a detailed description of each shot. But what you can do is write down a plan of action and what you expect to get out of the scene, or event.

Abbreviations

In order to help describe shots there is a conventional set of abbreviations to indicate the size of a shot, usually with reference to the human body, or buildings, or landscape, and also to indicate such things as whether the shot is indoors or outdoors.

- **LS** (long shot), showing the whole setting, or group of people.

- **MS** (medium shot), from the waist up with people, or a more detailed view of a building.

- **CS** (close shot), usually head and shoulders, or an architectural detail.

- **BCU** (big close up), where a head may be cropped top and bottom.

- **EXT** or **INT**, an outdoor shot or an indoor shot, whether by daylight or artificial light.

Other phrases frequently used are:

- **NIGHT EXT**, an outdoor scene shot at night.

- **DAY FOR NIGHT**, a scene shot to look like night, but actually shot during the day.

- **VO** (voice over), to indicate commentary or other voice track, accompanying the picture.

- **POV** (point of view) shot taken from the viewpoint of a participant, or of the audience.

- **PAN**, swivelling the camera horizontally.

- **TILT**, swivelling the camera vertically.

- **TRACK**, the camera is moved horizontally in any direction during the shot.

- **CRANE**, the camera is raised or lowered during the shot.

- **ZOOM IN** or **OUT**, the camera's zoom lens alters the shot size, as opposed to moving the camera nearer or further away.

- **CUT**, one shot ends and another begins with nothing in between.

- **DISSOLVE**, one shot fades away while at the same time the following shot fades in.

Laying out a shooting script

A good way of laying out a shooting script on A4 paper is to put the visuals on the left, with scene number and appropriate shot descriptions, and the audio material on the right (see the example in Figure 3).

Having the visuals and audio staggered in this way leaves plenty of space for notes to be added later. However, you may need a special programme if using a computer to get this layout.

Alternatively you can put the visuals all the way across the page and the accompanying audio directly underneath, as in Figure 4.

Some people find this easier to read, but it lacks the sense of visuals and audio flowing together and there is less space for notes.

You could identify the following requirements from this sample script:

1. A large office with several desks will be required.

2. Some lighting will probably be needed, since it is indoors, to boost the natural daylight.

3. Tracks will be needed to move the camera, or else a pan could be substituted if tracks are beyond the budget.

4. Tea will need to be available.

5. Old-fashioned typewriters will have to be found.

6. Music copyright clearance will be needed.

So as well as detailing the content and flow of your video, the shooting script will give the production scheduler, the cameraperson and the sound recordist information which they will need.

SCENE No. 6

DAY INT, SCRIPTWRITERS'
OFFICE

LS of office looking
towards windows.

CUs of writers at work,
typing on old-fashioned
typewriters.

At some point camera TRACKS
with a SECRETARY bringing
in cups of tea on a tray,
placing a cup beside each
writer.

> NARRATOR. In the old days a
> scriptwriter was part of a team.
> There could be as many as three
> or four writers engaged on one
> project.
>
> MUSIC from *Gone With the Wind*
> fades up over sound of clattering
> typewriters.

Fig. 3. Extract from the shooting script for *Those Golden Days*.

A shooting script is essential, both as a planning reference and as a framework for shooting, which you can alter if events demand it. Without one anarchy prevails!

SCENE No. 6

VISUAL

DAY INT, SCRIPTWRITERS' OFFICE.

LS of office looking towards windows.

CUs of writers at work, typing on old-fashioned typewriters.

At some point camera TRACKS with a SECRETARY bringing in cups of tea on a tray, placing a cup beside each writer.

AUDIO

NARRATOR. In the old days a scriptwriter was part of a team. There could be as many as three or four writers engaged on one project.

MUSIC from *Gone With the Wind* fades up over sound of clattering typewriters.

Fig. 4. Alternative layout for shooting script.

CHECKLIST

1. Define the purpose.

2. Research the subject.

3. Consider narrative possibilities.

4. Write outline treatment.

5. Flesh it out.

6. Prepare a shooting script.

4
Funding and Budgeting

INTRODUCTION

There are two ways of approaching this. Either you can ask yourself,

'I have x thousand pounds available. What can I achieve with that amount?'

or you can ask yourself,

'This is my script. How much money will I need to realise it?'

Which approach you adopt will depend on your circumstances. You might be part of a corporation with an annual video budget, or you might be someone with a burning desire to make that video and who will need to look for funds.

FINDING THE MONEY

If you don't have access to funds already, you have several possibilities.

Using your own
If the project is small in scale, like a family wedding, and you can use domestic equipment, it should not be unduly expensive. But as soon as you need to hire in equipment and expertise you will think twice about digging into your own pocket. Making a video is more expensive than writing a book. And once the video is made there is then the additional cost of making sufficient copies.

Searching for grants
You may be able to apply for a grant to make a video which would

fall within the remit of the organisation giving the grants.

Local authorities in the United Kingdom sometimes have funds available, usually in the departments dealing with the arts or social services, and there are also Regional Arts Boards and Production Funds for financing development, production and even exhibition. The BFI (British Film Institute) *Film and Television Handbook*, published annually, has a list of such organisations, with details of what they cover, in the section on Funding (see Useful Addresses).

In the United States it is often possible to approach philanthropic foundations set up to promote various causes, but this is less common in the United Kingdom where there are fewer private foundations, and those there are tend not to be especially enthusiastic about videos. Lists of foundations and charitable organisations can be found in the reference section of your local public library.

Seeking sponsorship

You may be able to find a sponsor to put up all or part of the money, perhaps in return for a mention in the credits. If you were a surgeon, for instance, with a new technique for treating a condition which involved the use of a drug, you may be able to persuade the drug company to finance the video. But as with all sponsorship, there may well be strings attached in terms of editorial control.

Trying television

If you think your project has a chance with television, including cable and satellite, you will need to approach the commissioning editor who deals with your particular subject matter, either directly yourself or through a production company or agent willing to handle your project, and preferably already known to the commissioning editor.

A commissioning editor will normally work to an annual budget which will be allotted to various projects due to be aired during a certain number of hours, or slots. Most likely some of these projects will not be entirely funded by the television station, but will rely on additional funding, perhaps from a distributor who may be able to sell the video to other outlets. Sponsorship money may also provide part of the funding, but this will depend on the rules about sponsorship, or 'indirect advertising', governing the television station, and this will vary in different countries.

Approaching distributors and workshops

It is difficult to get cash up front from a possible distributor of your video, but there are a number of distributors who are also workshops.

They aim to help an independent video-maker with cheap facilities or equipment, as well as a distribution set up, and they sometimes enter into co-production arrangements with projects which are 'up their street'. So if you think your project is not very commercial in the money-making sense, it would be well worth your while to approach one of these. There is a list of distributors and workshops in the United Kingdom in the Useful Addresses section.

AVOIDING TROUBLE

There are financial traps for the unwary in trying to fund a video.

Remaining solvent

If you need to spend money on hiring equipment, buying stock or paying people, make sure you are going to be refunded, unless you plan to finance it yourself. Unless you are an employee of a company or institution that wants the video, you should have some form of contract, or else arrange that all facilities will be ordered and paid for by your sponsor under your guidance.

Example: losing your sponsor
A charitable organisation has taken up your idea for a video. The chairman, a Mr W. E. Dogood, who has taken a personal interest in the project, has agreed to a budget of £5,000. You have hired equipment and bought stock and employed a cameraperson and recordist to the tune of £2,000, and shot some wonderful material. Unexpectedly, Mr W. E. Dogood dies of a heart attack. His job is taken over by a Mr I. G. Norit, who turns out to have no interest whatever in the project and feels no obligation to honour any arrangements made between you and his predecessor.

You have no written contract, and are faced with bills to be paid. You are probably unwilling to face a protracted legal battle centred on verbal contracts which you may well not win... Let's leave it unfinished!

Protecting your position
An alternative to the above is to form a limited company specifically for the making of the video. Then if something like that scenario does happen, your limited company will become insolvent and be wound up, but you and your family will survive. However, it costs money to form a limited company, and if it is wound up you may gain a bad reputation.

A better arrangement is for the sponsoring organisation to place money in an account with your bank. It can be placed there in stages to cover in advance each step in the project, such as development, pre-production, shooting, editing (post-production). If necessary you and the organisation can arrange for more than one signature to be required on cheques going out.

Negotiating co-funding

You may have half the money 'up front', from a television company for example, and a promise of the rest from another organisation whose annual budget has been used up. Because you are covering a unique event, you need to start shooting before the second half of the money becomes available. So you will need to get a promissory letter, which will satisfy the bank manager, enabling you to obtain a loan, to cover the full costs of production.

Co-ordinating funding from several sources may also involve you in a kind of juggling game where one organisation says they will put up some of the money, but only if a distributor, for instance, has already made a commitment to part fund the project. The distributor in turn may only be prepared to back the project if the other organisation has already made a commitment. How do you get either one of them to make the first move? A mixture of persuasion and being economical with the truth is one way!

Taking out insurance

Even if you are only hiring a camcorder for the weekend, make sure you have insurance against the possibility of it being stolen, and make sure you know what the exclusions are. You won't be covered against hazardous use, such as filming motor bike racing, without special arrangements.

With more complex projects it is essential to have Public Liability Insurance. If you are handling the project yourself then *you* must have it, otherwise the company you work for, or the production company you are working with, must have it. Without it you lay yourself open to being sued by anyone who might be a victim of an accident during shooting.

You can also insure against other eventualities, such as damage to, or loss of, your shot material. Having to reshoot a sequence can be very expensive when equipment has to be rehired, people re-engaged, travel rearranged, and so on. It is usually possible to arrange an insurance policy for the project which will cover such things. But it won't come cheap. There is a list of specialist companies handling such business under Useful Addresses

COSTING

If you have funding available, you will need to know what you can do with that amount of money, and if you are looking for funding you will need to know how much your project is going to cost. Most organisations will want to see a detailed budget before they let you spend their money. So you will need to do a budget.

Budget headings

There is no fixed way of doing a budget, but most people find it convenient to use some sort of formula which divides up the costs into sections. This makes it easier not to forget an item of expenditure, and also makes it easier to readjust the distribution of money between different items. You might, for instance, decide to cut back on shooting days in order to have more time for editing, and with a well layed out budget sheet you can see at a glance the amounts involved.

Below are suggested budget headings followed by a sample budget.

Production staff

In a commercial set-up this will include the fees of producer and director, scriptwriter, researcher, production manager, and anyone else involved in the project from beginning to end. The fees of a narrator or a composer would also be included under this heading.

Of course, with a non-commercial project, the above functions may well be combined in one or two people with zero remuneration, or your colleagues may already be on the payroll of a company. Even the narrator, perhaps a well-known actor, may be giving his services for nothing.

Crew costs

This should include the cost of hiring the equipment as well as people, like cameraperson, sound recordist, lighting technician, grip, etc. If you plan to use professional technicians, you should find out what the going rates are from BECTU (Broadcasting Entertainment Cinema & Television Union), or from a facilities company that hires out equipment and crew. These rates may be for an eight-hour day, or a ten-hour day, with additional amounts per hour for overtime. With an unpredictable subject, like filming a birth for instance, it is sometimes possible to negotiate an 'all in deal' for however many hours it may take.

It is often possible to do deals on hiring the camcorder and other equipment such as lights and sound recording gear, but you should budget for what you know you can get it for, not what you think you might be able to get it for.

Stock and processing (see also Chapters 6 and 7)

1. *Shooting on tape.* This covers tape cassettes required for shooting, and also the transfer cassettes used in the editing process, both for viewing at home, and in the edit suite. Do not forget audio tapes which you may use during research or for transcribing interviews once they are shot. You should include not only the physical tape cost, but also the cost of transfer, usually quoted as so much per hour. This will be considerably more than the actual tape cost.

2. *Shooting on film.* Include the cost of buying the rolls of film, usually quoted as so much per 400ft roll, and the cost of audio tape stock. Then put in the cost of developing the film in a laboratory, usually quoted as so many pence per foot. If you are going to edit on tape, there will also be the cost of telecine transfer of the developed negative and sound to your chosen tape format, and the cost of making transfers from that for viewing and editing. If editing on film then there will be the cost of making a work print from the developed negative, and the cost of sound transfers to a working sound format.

Preparation

Under this heading come all the travel, food and accommodation costs, not only during preparation when doing 'recces' of suitable locations, or researching interviewees, but also when shooting. You should include all sorts of diverse costs such as:

- petrol (gas)
- mileage
- car hire
- train or air fares
- meals
- hotels or other accommodation
- paying 'fixers' or 'minders'
- facility fees
- miscellaneous props.

Post-production
All the costs of the editing stage come here, notably:

- editor's fee, both off line and on line

- hire of off-line edit suite, or film cutting room with all its equipment

- tape and transfer costs incurred during the editing stage such as commentary or music

- commentary/music recording, including musicians' fees and copyright clearance

- hire of an on-line edit suite, or if working on film, cost of cutting negative to match work print, cost of trial print (answer print) from cut negative, and re-recording (dubbing) of sound track.

Delivery
Include the cost of transfer to the final format. If you have shot and edited on film but are going to distribute video copies, there will be a telecine transfer cost to make a suitable master tape from which cassettes for distribution can be made.

Do not forget the cost of copies for distribution. There is no point in completing a superb master tape of your project if no one can see it because there is no money left to make copies!

You may also need to include the cost of packaging your copies – having labels printed, for instance.

Overheads
Hopefully this item will be the least of your worries. But if you employ a secretary who might be involved in your video, that might count as an overhead. Include also:

- telephone calls
- faxes
- postage
- stationery
- courier services.

Insurance
As mentioned above under 'avoiding trouble', you will probably need to take out some kind of insurance. The cost is usually worked out as a percentage of the total budget.

Contingency
Some of your shooting may be crucially dependent on the weather, and if you are unlucky you may find you need another day's shooting. This would be an extra cost which could not be covered by insurance, so if you think contingencies are a possibility you should put in an amount under this heading to allow for extra shooting.

Sample budget

(See Figure 5.) Many of the items in this sample budget may not apply to your project, and the amounts are based roughly on commercial rates. You may be able to do all sorts of deals, or get reduced rates from a workshop. But you should at least ask yourself whether the items mentioned will apply to your project. Then you will be less likely to overlook a cost later on.

The most important costs to ascertain are the cost of a day's shooting, and the cost of a day's editing. Then you can figure out how many days shooting and editing you can afford with a given budget.

SCHEDULING

The shooting schedule is the essential companion to the shooting script (see Chapter 3). Having balanced a budget against the demands of the script, you now need to work out the most efficient and cost-effective plan for the shooting. The more locations there are the more complex this will be. Economy of time and travel will have to be balanced against the availability of participants.

There is always a temptation to try and cram too much into one day, particularly when a crew is involved. You need to allow for time to find parking, and for getting equipment in and out of buildings, as well as time for chit chat and maybe a cup of tea to help interviewees relax.

The other temptation to be resisted is to cut down on editing time. Of course, if your project is relatively straightforward and tightly scripted with controlled shooting conditions, you may not need much time in the edit suite. But with any project which involves shooting things as they happen – and this can include interviews – your shot material will rarely match up exactly with your shooting script. This means you will need time in the edit suite to work out alternative ways of using your material to get the result you want. So, unless you are stuck with a deadline delivery date, it is well worth scheduling your editing time in a way that gives you time to think. You may be able to arrange for periods of editing time with gaps in between, par-

Production company: Fly By Night Ltd
Project: 'Night Flying'

	£
Personnel:	
Salaries of producer/director, researcher, writer	6,000
Narrator	500
Composer	500
Production manager (part-time)	1,000
Crew Costs:	
Cameraperson 5 days at £200 per day	1,000
Sound recordist 5 days at £160 per day,	800
Hire of camcorder, lights and microphones,	
5 days at £200 per day	1,000
Stock and Processing:	
Tape stock 6 × 30min Beta SP tapes at £18 each	108
Transfers to VHS rushes at £10 per tape	60
Preparation:	
Accommodation for 4 people for 6 nights	480
Meals	250
Total mileage 300 at 30p per mile	90
Rail fares	50
Post-production:	
Editor, 2 weeks at £900 per week	1,800
Hire of off-line edit facilities, 9 days	
at £100 per day	900
Hire of on-line suite, 1 day	350
Transfers	150
Delivery:	
100 VHS copies at £8 per copy	800
Presentation cassettes, printing	100
Overheads:	
Telephone, fax	250
Postage, stationery	100
Bikes	50
Insurance:	
Production insurance	400
Contingencies:	
Based on 1 day's shooting	900
Total	17,638

Figure 5. Sample budget.

ticularly if the editor is involved in other projects besides yours. A seemingly intractable structural problem may be easily solved after a few days away from the edit suite.

Making up a call sheet

Everyone involved in the shooting should have a copy of the call sheet in advance of a day's shooting. You should always try to include the following information on it:

- The scene reference numbers for that day's shooting.

- The date and day of the week.

- Names of crew and any actors involved, with their telephone numbers.

- Full address of locations with photocopies of street maps and any useful instructions for finding it.

- Names and telephone numbers of contacts at the locations.

- Details of any catering arrangements (always reassuring to a crew!) or overnight accommodation.

- Details of rail or air travel arrangements.

- Details of any specially hired equipment and where it comes from.

- Details of any props or wardrobe required.

- Instructions as to what to do with the shot material, and who is responsible for it, at the end of the day (so it doesn't get lost!).

Some of this may seem like unnecessary nannying, but if everyone involved feels that the shoot has been efficiently organised, then you will get better co-operation and fewer logistical hitches.

CHECKLIST

1. You will most likely find yourself doing a juggling act with funding, scripting and budgeting, trying to match how much money you can get with what you want to do.

2. Always make sure you have taken all the necessary precautions against personal financial loss before you start spending, so check:

- contracts
- insurance
- money up front.

3. Inspire confidence in those working with you by drawing up efficient call sheets.

5
Getting Access to your Subject

PERSUADING

Any training you may have had in psychology or diplomacy will come in useful. Even where your subject is 'captive', that is to say where they are going to be filmed whether they like it or not because the boss says so, you will still need willing co-operation for a successful shoot. And where you are trying to persuade a person or an institution to let you film them, particularly if you are investigating a controversial issue, you may need to spend many hours in gentle coaxing and persuasion.

Persuading people
Start off by asking your prospective participant what their views about your project are, emphasising that you are an interested inquirer, even though you may already have formed your own opinions. You can then move on to explain that their participation will be important to the success of your video. Most people are surprisingly willing to take part in something which may be for them a bit out of the ordinary.

Once you have gained their trust you should not neglect to inform them of the extent of any disruption in their home or office which the shooting may cause. Some people may assume that you will be the only one involved in the shooting, and when unexpectedly faced with a crew and lights, no matter how discreet, they may then refuse to participate.

Persuading organisations
Here you may have to deal with the bad impressions left by those who came before. 'We had a TV crew in here last year, never again', they might say. They might have at least two reasons for saying this:

1. The crew caused disruptions, broke things, or caused a power failure with loss of production and computer shut down.

2. The organisation was shown in an unfavourable light.

On the other hand, you may be lucky if your predecessors set an excellent example! You may have an advantage if you can show that you are not a professional media person making a television programme. But you will certainly be closely questioned as to your motives and reasons for wanting to film within their organisation, and you will need all your diplomatic skills to overcome initial reluctance.

Example: the Royal Opera House
A recent example of an investigative project about an organisation was the BBC (British Broadcasting Corporation) documentary series *The House*, about the inner workings and power struggles at the Royal Opera House in London. This involved many months of patient discussions, persuasion and negotiation, not only before shooting, but during shooting as well. One of the key factors in getting permission for the project was the idea that it could well be in the long-term interests of the organisation for its inner workings to be revealed, even if it did cause some controversy. To put such an idea to an organisation can be a delicate task!

Securing editorial control
You may find that a prospective interviewee or organisation will agree to take part only if they have editorial control, that is to say only if they have the right to cut out parts of their interview or other material which they feel might put them at a disadvantage in the context of your final editing.

This is most likely to occur if you have failed to build up a relationship of trust with the participant, and it is a sign of trouble to come! The traditional approach in television is to refuse to grant editorial control in virtually all situations. If it were otherwise, it is easy to see that many participants would simply manipulate television to their own advantage.

However, you should make it clear that you are prepared to consider any points or problems raised by the participant, and that you would be prepared to make changes so long as your intentions are not compromised.

GETTING PERMISSION

You will usually need to get permission if you intend filming on public or private property, and sometimes if you intend to include people. Even if you already know the person in charge it still pays to ask their permission, and at the same time you can make sure there is no other event happening which might interfere with your shooting.

Places
You are likely to need permission to shoot in the following situations:

- parks and nature reserves
- stations
- airports
- palaces
- hospitals and surgeries
- shops and supermarkets
- people's houses
- factories
- churches
- clubs
- cafés and restaurants
- schools and colleges
- holiday resorts
- swimming pools and stadiums.

If you look anything like a professional video or film unit, with a tripod, and sound recordist, and maybe a battery light, you will almost certainly be asked if you have written permission. If you haven't, and you don't even know the name of the person in charge, you will be asked to leave, or move on. In some countries permission to film in public places is strictly controlled by government agencies who may want to see your script. Many governments and organisations have become highly sensitive to film and video units as a result of the transmission on television of not always favourable documentaries investigating their activities.

Busking it
There may be occasions when you are refused permission, or when you do not wish to alert the relevant authority to what you are doing. The more you look like a tourist with a domestic camcorder, the more likely you are to get away with at least enough time to get the most important shots before you are thrown out. But in some countries you could find yourself accused of spying, or have your tape confiscated.

People

Even though you have the agreement of a participant to appear and speak in your video, you may still need other people's permission.

Example: filming in school

You are making a video about a handicapped child in school. You will need not only the child's permission, but also the parent's and the teacher's, and the headmaster's, and possibly even that of the parents of other children in the same class.

Sometimes it is sufficient simply to ask if there is anyone who does not wish to appear in the video and then to take whatever steps are necessary in the shooting and editing to ensure they are not seen in the final result.

Release forms

If your video is likely to have any kind of public showing, and certainly if it is to be shown on television, you should get each participant, or interviewee, to sign a form known as a release form, which will protect you, or whoever shows your video, should the interviewee subsequently decide to take legal action against you because they have changed their minds, or don't like the context in which they have appeared. So as not to alarm them with legal forms, the best time to get them to sign is just after you have finished interviewing them, emphasising that it is just a formality, which in most cases it is!

Typically, the wording should be something like the example in Figure 6.

In the United States such a form is only valid with a token one dollar payment to the interviewee. If a fee is involved you can add, 'In consideration of the sum of £ ... now paid to me (receipt of which is hereby acknowledged)' to go before 'I agree', and so on.

Following up permission

Once you have obtained verbal permission to shoot somewhere, do not assume that all will go smoothly. A frequent scenario is for a video crew to turn up on the appointed day only to find that the man on the gate knows nothing about it, and the person you spoke to originally is off sick or on holiday, and the replacement was not told.

So always send a letter or memo confirming the arrangements that were made, and perhaps add a polite request such as, 'please inform security that we will need access to the back entrance with equipment, and parking space.'

You should also telephone a day or two ahead of the time you are

TO: Mr A. Videomaker
DATE: 1 October 199X
Dear Sirs,

I agree to the recording and broadcasting of the interview given by me to you on ..... and hereby give all consents necessary for the reproduction, exhibition, transmission, broadcast and exploitation thereof without time limit throughout the universe by all means and media (whether known or hereafter invented) without liability or acknowledgement to me.

You shall be entitled to cut and edit the interview as you deem fit and you shall not be obliged to include all or any of the same in any programme.

Yours faithfully

Name.................   Signed.................

Address ....
       ....
       ....
       ....

Figure 6. Release form.

due to shoot. You can say that you are telephoning to make sure it is still convenient for them, even though your real reason is to make sure they haven't forgotten.

CHECKLIST

1. Don't compromise your integrity by giving away editorial control. You need to remain in charge.

2. Make sure you have relevant permissions and release forms before shooting.

3. Be patient and diplomatic with tricky subjects.

6
Using Actors and Real People

REASONS FOR USING ACTORS

1. It might be advantageous to have a well-known actor or actress to be a presenter in your video, or simply to read the commentary. Many actors are prepared to donate their services free of charge for a charity with which they can feel associated.

2. You may need to recreate an event, or even an 'interview', where it is not possible to shoot the actual situation, either because it has already happened, or the people are no longer living. There are also situations where you may feel you can't ask someone to appear on camera to 'relive' a traumatic experience, and using an actor to give an interview based on what the actual person said to you would be a way round this difficulty.

3. You may have decided that scripting a drama situation for at least part of your video would be the most effective way of getting your message across. The most obvious examples of this are corporate training videos.

FINDING ACTORS

Unless you already have someone in mind, the best way to start looking is to get hold of a copy of *Spotlight*, the actors' directory. This has photographs of most leading actors and actresses, and also character actors and the less well-known, with some details of their roles, and who their agent is. You can than contact the agents of likely candidates to see:

1. Whether the actor or actress might be interested in your project.

2. Whether they might be available.

3. What they would cost.

A less formal alternative is to contact your local amateur dramatic society to see if there is anyone with some acting experience who might be willing to take part in your video. You might be surprised to find how much untapped talent there is out there.

DEALING WITH ACTORS

If you are proposing to use professional actors with lines to deliver in a scripted dramatic situation, then you should use the services of a professional director. Unless you have directing experience in the theatre, or you are an actor yourself, you would soon find yourself well out of your depth. A reputable actor's agent will want to know what *your* experience is, and who is going to be directing.

Selecting actors

You and your director may have a short list of candidates, and the best way to choose is to arrange an audition in a suitable venue such as a hall or large reception room, away from too much noise. You can then interview each candidate, explaining your project to them, and your director can ask them to read a piece of the script, or to improvise a situation.

Remember that actors are very vulnerable people, so treat them with respect. Even if you have already decided that the first candidate is ideal, you should still assess them all with equal attention, since they have taken the trouble to come and be auditioned. You may also have second thoughts on further reflection.

Presenters and commentators

If you are planning to use a well-known actor to 'front' a charity video, for example, you would not normally need to use a professional director. The actor or actress will be thoroughly professional, and well aware of what the camera is doing. Your main job will be to:

- make them welcome

- be hospitable

- arrange their transport

- make sure they have your script well in advance of the shooting date

- make sure all the equipment is ready and working.

GETTING PERFORMANCES FROM REAL PEOPLE

Much of your visual material, over which you may use voice over from an interview, or music, will consist of participants doing what they normally do in their job or leisure time. Getting a good 'performance' from them amounts to making sure they *don't* try to perform or 'act up' for your benefit. If they become at all self-conscious they will come over as 'acting up' and give a bad performance.

Your role is to make them feel at ease rather than to direct them. You will need to keep the presence of the camera crew, and lights, as unobtrusive as possible. It is particularly important if you are asking your participant to 'be natural' in front of their colleagues or friends.

Example: the vicar's wife makes tea
You want to shoot Mrs Wellbeloved, the vicar's wife, making tea for one of the widowed parishioners. Rather than directing her to fill the kettle, switch it on, put some tea in the teapot, get the milk out of the fridge, and so on, you could simply say, 'We could do with a break. Can you make us all a cup of tea, and we'll film you while you're doing it.' Nine times out of ten you will have a perfect take.

CHECKLIST

1. Treat actors with respect, and use a professional director for drama scripts.

2. If you ask a person to do something they are used to doing, and they see a purpose in it, and you have their trust, you will seldom go wrong.

7
Shooting It

GETTING THE BEST IMAGE QUALITY

Perhaps you remember, or your grandparents would remember, the earlier days of photography when the family camera was something like a 'box brownie' with a cheap lens which you didn't have to focus, and a 'dull' and 'bright' setting. Technically the image quality was poor, but it didn't matter much since the prints were small, for the family album.

At the same time there were photographers like Ansel Adams and others who were using large and sophisticated cameras mounted on tripods and recording on huge negatives. These produced images capable of yielding gigantic high definition enlargements.

The first was cheap, the second was expensive. We have the same kind of choice with video.

Factors affecting image quality
Resolution
The amount of fine detail which can be recorded depends on how good the lens is and also on how good the recording medium is. In the case of video the cheaper systems will only have something like 240 horizontal lines in the frame from which to construct the image, whereas a broadcast quality system will have around 600 or even 1,100 such lines. Obviously there is no point in using a high quality expensive lens on a 'domestic' recording system with only 240 lines – the benefits of the lens would be wasted.

Contrast
Even though the resolution is good, the picture might look flat and muddy, or on the other hand it might look like soot and whitewash. A poor lens will degrade the contrast. A cheaper recording system will not be able to handle extremes of light and shadow in the subject so well as a more expensive one.

Colour
We judge colour images by how accurately a colour is reproduced, but whether we find it pleasing or not is a very subjective matter. The cheaper video systems tend to reproduce colours rather crudely, particularly strong reds, which can even 'bleed' into other areas of colour. The higher quality systems record the colour signal separately from the 'light and dark' signal, which makes for more accurate colours, and also more scope for subtly adjusting them in post-production.

Lighting
Image quality can be greatly improved by good lighting – all the more important with the cheaper cameras. It will not increase the resolution, the amount of fine detail that can be recorded, but it can make it more 'readable' to the eye.

Duplication
This becomes relevant in the editing stages. Each time you make an analogue copy of a video tape, the resolution, the contrast and the colour will all deteriorate to some extent, and copies from copies will look worse and worse. The number of 'generations' is strictly limited before image quality becomes unacceptable. Starting off with a high quality original will ensure that copies show minimum deterioration.

The only way to avoid deterioration is to copy digitally, and as far as editing is concerned this means using digital editing equipment (see Chapter 8, editing systems).

Does image quality matter?
The answer to this question is first of all to ask another question – does your project matter? You may think that the important thing is to get your message across, and you would be right. But if you watched a poorly shot, fuzzy looking commercial with bleeding colours, trying to sell you a holiday in some exotic place, you would be disinclined to take up the offer. There will always be an inevitable connection in the viewer's mind between the quality of the image (and let us not forget the sound) and the quality of the product or message.

Of course, the limiting factor is cost, but the aim is to get the best image quality consistent with the expected viewing conditions. A technically very high image quality will be required if your film is to be projected onto a large cinema screen, but there is no point in having an image quality far beyond what is required for domestic television viewing. The image quality to aim for depends on your expected outlet. This could be:

- VHS copies privately distributed for home viewing

- corporate viewing with large conference TV screens

- broadcast television, where there are usually minimum technical standards laid down

- the Empire Leicester Square, or equivalent big screen cinema.

Case study: 'domestic quality' lets you down

A local factory has been taken over and many workers made redundant, bringing economic disaster and hardship to the community. You feel that this injustice cannot go unrecorded, and you decide to make a video documentary about it. You have trouble finding money to hire equipment, but your rich cousin offers you the use of his domestic Hi-8 camcorder. You decide to go ahead with that, thinking the TV company are bound to take it for showing, since it is such a 'hot' subject.

You present them with the finished video and they turn it down, saying it does not meet their technical standards for broadcasting. Your spies tell you that the real reason it was turned down was because the TV company were being leaned on by the big corporation, who didn't want it shown. You gave the TV company the perfect excuse for not showing it by using domestic instead of broadcast quality.

This kind of situation is always a tricky one, but it is well worth aiming for the required technical image quality, if only to reassure yourself as to the real reasons for a refusal.

Remembering the key points

1. Aim for the best image quality you can afford related to the expected viewing.

2. Remember that image quality will always affect the viewer's perception of your message or product.

CHOOSING A FORMAT

Video technology is developing at an ever faster rate, not only in the areas of storage, editing and transmission, but also the camcorders themselves are getting smaller and delivering better pictures. However, camcorders still use tape cassettes, including moving parts. Disk editing and storage is now feasible, though expensive, but *recording* onto disk is not yet commercially feasible in most fields.

Unfortunately for the consumer, manufacturers seem to be more concerned about beating their rivals to the marketplace than about developing a world-wide standard format, so there are now quite a number of different tape formats in existence. But remember that the format you choose to shoot with need not be the same as the format you use for editing and exhibition. Listed below are the commonest tape formats currently in use. Also included is the option of originating on film, still capable of delivering quality images even better than the latest digital tape formats.

VHS

This is the format used in domestic players, and is also still used in camcorders, which can now be bought or hired quite cheaply. But the picture quality and sound are quite rudimentary in comparison to later developments, and the camcorder needs to be large enough to take the standard VHS cassette, although there are minicassette versions.

S-VHS

This is the same size as VHS and will give you superior quality, but needs to be used in an S-VHS camcorder to reap the benefits. The best S-VHS camcorders will deliver very good picture and sound, but it is not a 'hold it in your palm' format.

Recently a digital version of this format has emerged, known as *Digital S*, with a complete system of camcorders and editing equipment, all digital. Better, but more expensive.

U-matic

This is a larger tape size (¾ inch), and can be high band or low band. It's only worth thinking about if you already have access to U-matic equipment, in a college or corporate environment for instance. Otherwise as a format it has become somewhat outdated, and cameras and recorders are more cumbersome than S-VHS.

HI-8

The tape cassette is smaller, the tape is narrower, and yet the image and sound quality are far superior to VHS, and even better if used in one of the more expensive three-chip camcorders. The smaller cassette means that the camcorder is handier to shoot with in highly mobile or discreet situations.

Beta SP

SP stands for superior performance. This is the professional format most often used when television transmission is envisaged. It will give you the best quality of all the analogue tape formats so far mentioned, but the camcorder it's used in will be expensive to hire (around £300 per day with the usual accessories). It is also the tape format most often used for the master edit at the on-line suite (see Chapter 8), from which VHS copies can be made for distribution.

There is now a digital version of this format, known as *Digital Betacam*, with a camcorder to match, giving even better picture quality, and capable of being used in the wide screen or 'letterbox' image shape of future television sets, as well as the current standard image shape.

You will definitely need a large budget to be able to afford to shoot with these formats.

DV (Digital Video)

This is a more recent development in the consumer field, where sound and picture are recorded digitally, and it is set to supercede HI-8, being just as handy to operate and delivering better pictures. DVCAM and DVPRO are trade names for professional versions of the DV consumer format, but beware of incompatibility in certain respects. Compatible digital editing systems are now offered by the main manufacturers, but for the immediate future it's all expensive kit to buy or hire.

Film 16mm

Don't rule out the idea of using film to originate your video. It may sound like going back to the stone age, but with the advances in film emulsion technology the image quality is still superior, even to Beta-SP and digital broadcast quality camcorders. After all, the technology of photographic emulsions has been around since about 1830, more than 160 years, and has progressed further than the relatively recent video technology.

Also it may be easier to get the use of an older film camera, in which you can use the most up-to-date film emulsions.

Film Super 16mm

This is a wide-screen version of the standard 16mm film image. The negative area is stretched out to one side, increasing the recording area by about 40 per cent, achieved by eliminating the sprocket holes down that side, the overall dimensions of the film remaining the same.

Processing costs are the same as for standard 16mm. Older cameras have to be adapted, though modern ones incorporate it as a standard option. You also have to use a zoom lens which will cover the increased area without 'vignetting'. Worth thinking about if you anticipate showings on the widescreen HDTV (High Definition Television) systems now in the pipeline, or if you anticipate 'blow-ups' for cinema showings.

It's perhaps worth mentioning that quite a few of the more prestigious documentaries and dramas on television are still *shot*, but not necessarily edited, on 16mm or super 16mm, in preference to video.

Deciding between tape and film

If image quality is going to be an important consideration in your video, and you have a choice of originating on film or tape, here are some key points to help you make up your mind.

Advantages of tape
- You can check your shots immediately by playing back in the viewfinder or on a monitor.

- Tape is cheaper to buy and the cassettes last longer.

- Automatic exposure and colour balancing mean you don't have to have much photographic knowledge to operate most camcorders.

Advantages of film
- Superior image quality, even compared to digital tape formats.

- The latest film emulsions can be used in even quite old film cameras (including clockwork!).

- You can see through the lens to line up shots without power.

- Film cameras use less battery power.

- The sound recordist can operate completely independently of the camera.

- It will 'blow up' successfully for cinema showing.

Disadvantages of tape
- Video uses up batteries more quickly, and you need to switch on to line up a shot.

- You can waste a lot of time on a tight schedule playing back your material to check it.

- The sound recordist is umbilically tied to the camcorder, which can be awkward in mobile situations.

- Picture quality will not be maintained if you try to 'blow up' for the cinema.

Disadvantages of film
- The magazines don't last as long (only ten minutes) as a tape cassette.

- Film stock is a lot more expensive than tape stock. (This would force you to think more carefully about what you really need to shoot – a possible plus point?)

- You need to know about photography to get good results, and you can't check results before processing.

Making the choice

At first sight you have a bewildering choice. Much depends on who you are targeting with your video and what facilities they will have to view it – domestic TV sets, conference screens, cinemas – as well as, of course, your budget.

For a simple record of an event, say a wedding or a new surgical operating technique or a trip abroad, standard VHS might be adequate. You can circulate a limited number of copies without too much quality deterioration. But if you anticipate a large number of copies, or television transmission, you should aim ideally to use Beta SP, or at least S-VHS. HI-8 or a digital format might also be acceptable. Remember that you can 'bump up' from a cheaper or more convenient, or more readily available, format for shooting, to a quality format like Beta SP for your edit.

It's also worth looking into the possibility of free or discounted film stock from Kodak or Fuji, if you think there is any possibility of them wanting to be associated with your project.

Convenience
If your shooting is relatively static with the camcorder on a tripod in controlled situations, then the bulkier VHS or S-VHS camcorders will not be a disadvantage. But if you need to be highly mobile or discreet you will need HI-8 or the new DV format.

Time coding
Only the professional camcorders are capable of putting professional time code (see below Using time code) on the tape for

frame-accurate editing. If you use domestic camcorders, and you plan to use professional editing facilities, time code will need to be put on at the beginning of the editing stage.

Digital claims
Beware of being seduced by exaggerated claims for picture quality in some of the new miniature DV camcorders appearing on the market. They may well be better than the analogue *equivalent*, but not necessarily better than, for instance, an analogue camcorder with three CCDs (Charged Coupled Devices), a superior lens and resolving more lines.

If you think you have the budget to 'go digital' you would be well advised to go for digital editing systems (see Chapter 8) in post-production, thus preserving the quality of your original material and benefiting from the convenience, rather than a digital camcorder (unless you can afford the lot!). There is little point in having a marginally superior camera original if the benefits are going to be lost in the copying stages of an analogue editing system.

TV systems

The unfortunate legacy of the early race to develop national television systems is that there are now two mutually incompatible originating systems, or 'standards'. These are:

1. **PAL (Phase Alternate Line)** used in the United Kingdom, much of Europe, Australia, India, Asia and parts of Africa.

2. **NTSC (National Television System Committee)** used in the United States, Canada, the Caribbean, parts of South America and parts of Asia, including Japan.

There is a third system, **SECAM (Sequential Colour and Memory)**, used in France and some other countries, which affects television transmission of the colour signal, although material is originated using PAL equipment.

The practical implications of this are that you cannot, for instance, play a PAL-recorded videotape in the United States, either on television or at home. Nor can you play an NTSC-recorded videotape on PAL or SECAM equipment. Camcorders sold in domestic markets will generally be built to function only with that country's system. However, some of the more sophisticated professional camcorders have interchangeable circuit boards to convert from one system to the other.

Converting
If you need to show copies of your video in a country with the other system, you will need to do a 'standards' conversion. Most video facilities companies (see Useful Addresses) are able to offer this service, but there will be a quality loss, as in any video copying, and it will be expensive. With SECAM you can usually succeed in playing a PAL tape by using the scart socket on more recent equipment.

Film
Film is compatible with *any* television system, in the sense that it can be transferred to tape and/or broadcast in any country without the necessity for conversion from one system to another.

Remembering the key points
1. Choice of format involves:

• cost

• eventual outlet

• desired image quality

• convenience of shooting.

2. Think twice about *shooting* digital, unless you can follow it through with digital editing.

3. Remember that you can shoot on one format and edit on another.

BUYING OR HIRING THE EQUIPMENT

You may already have free access to camcorders or cameras in your chosen format. Otherwise buying equipment, assuming you have the money, only makes sense if you think you can resell it for a reasonable price when you have finished with it, or if the cost of buying a relatively unsophisticated consumer camcorder is no more than what it would cost you to hire it over the shooting period.

In the current economic situation of most countries in Europe, and the USA, it is possible to negotiate quite good deals for hiring HI-8 or broadcast standard equipment, although it may not be the most up to date. Find a video or film facilities company or a workshop (some addresses are in the Useful Addresses section at the back of this book) who are sympathetic and willing to discuss your requirements. Be prepared to say how much you have in your budget for equipment hire.

Some companies may offer a deal for reduced rates of camera hire if you use their own editing facilities as well. Make sure this suits you before accepting, as you may already have access to free or very cheap editing facilities, or you might find yourself having to put up with what's on offer instead of being able to insist on what you want with a separate editing facility.

You may also be offered tape stock on the grounds that the company's equipment is lined up to suit a particular brand of tape. Before accepting, check whether you can get it cheaper elsewhere.

Lights, and sometimes transport, are often included in a package deal. Make sure that they are the sort that you want and that spare 'bubbles' (bulbs) are included. Make sure that lights, cables and plugs/sockets conform to safety regulations. Under forthcoming European law, lighting equipment for hire has to be stamped or verified as having been recently tested.

Insurance

If hiring, be careful to check the company's terms of business, and whether you are expected to take out insurance for the equipment, or whether you are paying them a supplement to cover insurance. You may also be asked whether you intend any hazardous use of the equipment. In any case, if you do intend to film anything hazardous, like mountaineering or car racing, you should say so and discuss whether any additional premium is required. See also Chapter 4 on insurance.

Remembering the key points

• Only buy if it makes good economic sense.

• Be careful of inclusive hire deals – you may not want it all.

• Check safety and insurance.

USING TIME CODE

The purpose of time code (TC) is to provide a filing system with rapid retrieval, to make editing more accurate, and to achieve synchronisation between separate camcorders or sound recorders being used simultaneously. Space is available on the magnetic tape not only for picture and sound recording but also for recording time code. There are several systems:

1. **RCTC (Recordable Consumer Time Code)**. This is like a clock, and is found in many domestic camcorders. It is quite useful if you

want to do simple editing on domestic linear editing equipment, but it is not accurate enough for use in professional editing facilities.

2. **SMPTE (Society of Motion Picture and Television Engineers).** This is based on the notion that there are thirty separate frames of picture every second. Thus every frame will have its own separate reference number, essential for accurate editing in a professional editing suite, and there are a sufficient number of digits to be able to record tape roll numbers, minutes and seconds, as well as frames.

3. **EBU (European Broadcasting Union).** This is a European version of the American SMPTE, based on twenty-five frames every second.

These last two can be used in either a free running mode, like a clock set going at the beginning of the shooting day, or in a record run mode, where the 'clock' only functions when the camera is recording. Using the first mode will tell you, for instance, at what time of day a shot was taken, but there will be big jumps in the recorded time code for the times when the camera was not recording. The machinery which 'reads' the time code in a digital editing suite prefers the second mode, which gives a continuous time code without gaps in the numbering.

User bits

This is an additional facility found on professional camcorders which allows you to record a set of digits to represent the date, or a roll number. The digits remain static until you readjust them. This information, like time code, is recorded separately from picture and sound.

Synchronising

Time code is also used for synchronising different recording devices. For instance, if you are shooting with film you can photographically record time code on the edge of the negative, and use it to synchronise the sound recorded on a separate machine, where both camera and sound recorder have had their 'clocks' set going together at the beginning of the day's shoot.

Similarly, if you need to record an event with more than one camcorder, they can all be set going with the same time code. In theory all the different time code clocks will tick at the same rate with no appreciable drift over several hours. In practice they should all be rechecked every two hours or so.

Clapper boards
These are used for synchronising when shooting on film, using a camera without time code. You can also use them with time code as a back up system in case there are problems with the time code.

They are simple to use, and visually identify the shot with a scene, and/or slate number, with the date and any other useful information. The camera sees the 'clap' close and the recordist picks up the sound of the clap. This will enable the film editor later on to synchronise sound and picture by picking out the frame where the clap closes and matching it to the frame on the sound track where the bang is.

If you are working with old-fashioned film technicians you may find that champagne is called for when reaching slate no. 100!

Checklist
1. Make sure the time code system you will be using will be compatible with the editing facilities you plan to use.

2. Remember to reset the time code with each new tape cassette.

3. Finally, remember that you don't have to have professional time code when shooting. It can be put on afterwards at the start of the editing process.

USING LIGHT

You will not be able to record an image in total darkness (except with x-ray or infra red), so you will need a certain minimum amount of light, depending on how sophisticated the format and camera system you intend to use is. This light may be present naturally as daylight or artificial light, or you may have to add your own light to augment it, in which case you need to check that there is sufficient mains electricity.

A second, and creatively more important, reason for using lights is to achieve a certain effect – to flatter your subject, to pretend the scene is lit by window light when in fact it isn't, to impart a mood: bright and cheerful or dark and sombre. Included in this idea is the possibility of placing the camera in a position where you can make use of an existing light, such as the sun, to get the effect you want. A 'talking head' front lit by the sun will be 'well lit' in the sense of having plenty of light on him/her, but he/she will probably squint, and a more pleasing result can be obtained by placing camera and subject so that the sun becomes a side or even a back light. So, the process of lighting can include positioning the camera as well as positioning lights.

Being discreet

If your video is going to involve people in their own homes, or doing their own thing in a club, in church, or wherever, then you will want to cause minimum disturbance with lights.

Don't use more than you need to get a satisfactory image, and avoid dazzling people. This will mean avoiding too much frontal lighting, which tends to look 'flat' anyway. Your pictures will generally look more interesting if side or back lit, and you can get quite a good fill light (to lighten the shadows) by bouncing off a white ceiling or wall.

When you have placed your lights, switch them on gradually to avoid disturbing the atmosphere, and switch them off gradually when you have finished. As Michael Rabiger says in *Directing the Documentary*, 'The discomfort caused by injudicious lighting serves to inhibit the nervous.'

Getting the colour right

Another aspect of light which has to be borne in mind is its colour temperature. You may remember from school physics that a blue flame is hotter than a yellow flame, measured in degrees Kelvin. Likewise daylight, which is predominantly blue from the sky, is measured as being around 5,000 degrees Kelvin, and tungsten light, which is yellower, as being 3,200 degrees Kelvin. Nevertheless we speak of daylight looking 'cooler', i.e. bluer, than tungsten light, probably because of our inbuilt psychological response to colours.

Most camcorders need to be shown something white in the light that is to be used, and they will then adjust themselves to give correct colour rendering (see section on white balancing on page 73). Some have pre-set switches for either daylight or tungsten light.

Bear in mind that tungsten lights can be made to give out 'daylight' by fitting blue gelatin or glass filters over the front.

Film
Whereas in camcorders you use the same tape whatever the light, with film stock you use either tungsten-balanced film or daylight-balanced film. The tungsten balanced film needs a conversion filter

over the lens (more or less orange) to be used in daylight, otherwise it would come out too blue.

Case study: filming in a mountain hut
A television programme for Channel Four called *Birds as Prey*, about shooting wood pigeon in the Pyrenees, involved filming in the con-servationist's outpost, a hut high in the mountains with no electric-ity, lit only by candles at night. The light level was insufficient to get quality images of people playing guitars, writing up their notes, and cooking supper.

Three 12 volt 100 watt halogen lamps hidden in the rafters illumi-nating key areas inside the hut gave just enough added light to be able to record, but without killing the effect of the candles. Electric current was supplied via a cable leading outside to the battery of a car parked a short distance away with its engine running.

The lamps were placed so that there would be a variety of possi-ble camera positions, some side, some back, and some front lit, which would all look like light from the existing candles. To lighten shad-ows on foreground faces there was an additional 12 volt 5 watt car sidelight bulb in a homemade lamp, run off the camera's battery.

With this set-up it was possible to capture all the required shots, including talking heads, without having to rearrange any lights, thereby causing minimal disturbance to the activities in the hut.

Using the jargon
Terms commonly used are :

- *High key* – bright overall lighting.

- *Low key* – lots of dark areas with pools or shafts of light, for dra-matic effect.

- *Hard* – where the main light source will cast a hard-edged shadow.

- *Soft* – a more diffuse light source, such as a window, casting a soft-edged shadow.

- *Mixed lighting* – when there are light sources of different colour temperature in the same scene, e.g. a cooler, or bluer, light from a window and a warmer light from a table lamp. Can be very effec-tive if kept subtle.

- *Magic hour* – that time immediately after the sun sets when there is still enough light in the sky (bluish) to record, often mixed with 'warm' street lights and illuminated windows. Note that this time is almost non-existent near the equator and much longer than an hour near the poles.

- *Practicals* – any light source included in the shot, such as a table lamp. You may need to substitute brighter or dimmer bulbs to harmonise with the rest of the lighting.

- *Day for night* – where a scene which is supposed to be at night according to the script is shot during the day and made to look like night by a combination of filtering and deliberate underexposure. May be cheaper (no overtime) and also enables more detail in the backgrounds to be seen without a lot of extra lights.

Checklist for possible locations
- Mains electricity?
- White ceilings?
- Daylight or artificial?
- Windows or skylights?
- Direction of sun?

RECORDING SOUND

This is where even some professional television programmes fall down. How often have you seen one of those 'fly on the wall' documentaries where you have to struggle to hear what someone is saying against a horrendous background noise?

Using microphones
Most camcorder mikes are unselective and merely record whatever sound is in front of them, sometimes even picking up the noise of the power zoom. Indeed all microphones are unselective in that, unlike the human ear, they do not psychologically filter out unwanted noise.

However, a good quality directional microphone can be used away from the camcorder to 'select' sound by positioning it to point at the sound that is wanted (so long as there is no unwanted sound in between), virtually eliminating sounds to the side or behind.

'Personal' microphones can be attached to a person's chest to record their speech. These are omnidirectional, but will record the speech much more prominently than surrounding background noise. However, they also tend to pick up clothing rustle, and you need to monitor the sound to be aware of it. You also need to be discreet when attaching them, particularly if you want to hide the cable behind clothing.

Using a recordist

If your video is going to need anything more ambitious than simple 'social event' talk from the camcorder microphone, you are strongly advised to get someone with at least a basic knowledge of sound recording, who knows how to deploy microphones to get the best possible sound quality. This may well mean sometimes restricting the visual freedom of the camera so as to avoid microphones in shot, for the sake of good sound. Such a person can also monitor the sound through headphones, and adjust levels manually instead of having to rely on the 'automatic record' facility.

Anticipating the edit

Think about recording sound tracks to be used to lay over pictures later, in the editing. If you want to use the speech track from a 'talking head' interview to lay over other images, you will only be able to do this successfully if there is no obtrusive background sound recorded with the speech at the time of shooting. Remember there is no affordable magic for separating the background noise from the speech once it's been recorded. Some background noise may be acceptable in an interview if it relates to the visual background of the shot, but it certainly won't be acceptable if used over other images.

Example: a factory worker in a noisy bottling plant being interviewed next to his machine about his holiday dreams.
It occurs to you later, in the editing, to use some of his sentences over dreamlike shots of Caribbean beaches with the gentle sound of waves and calypso music. Even if his words are intelligible in the factory context, the whole effect with the beach shots would be ruined by the machinery noise which is there with the words. *Solution*: foresee the possibility and record at least some of the appropriate speech as a separate sound track in a quiet room. Not always easy to organise and will involve scheduling (see page 40).

Planning ahead and careful checking
If you are using a recordist remember to tell them that you might want to use the speech track over other images in the edit, otherwise they may assume you are happy with the background noise.

Even when shooting an interview in a quiet room you should still record a minute or so of the sound of the 'quiet room' (called *room tone* or *buzz track*), to be used later on for smoothing over any changes in the background sound which may become apparent when you make cuts in the interview.

Finally, it's always worth checking on whether there might be a road-mending crew drilling outside your location on the day you plan to shoot.

Remembering the key points

1. A microphone will record all the sound that is presented to it, including sounds you may not want.

2. Sound quality is as important, and sometimes more so, than picture quality.

3. Make your video better than most by making sure that sound is thought about in advance of shooting.

USING A CREW

If you are planning to make a video which is anything more than a simple record of a wedding or family holiday, you will need help (see Chapter 1). The more controlling you have to do in terms of cajoling people to co-operate, chatting up participants, and simply trying to keep your eye on the ball as far as your script is concerned, the more likely it is that you will need to delegate the visual and sound recording functions, and even the administrative functions of transport, food and lodging.

You may have a budget to hire professionals, or you may be relying on volunteers, or the help of colleagues. Whoever they are you will have to gain their trust and respect.

Choosing people

Professionals may come as part of a package with the equipment from a facilities company, or they may be freelance individuals. Although it may be safe to assume that they are technically competent as camerapersons or sound recordists, you should nevertheless try and meet them first, or at least chat on the phone, to see whether they are likely to be sympathetic towards your project. It's no good using someone who turns out to have racist attitudes if you are making a video about ethnic communities.

Unless you already know a sound recordist, it's a good idea to leave that choice to the cameraperson. They need to get on well in order to co-operate over the inevitable compromises necessary to get good sound and good picture, and if they have worked together before it's a big plus.

A professional cameraperson will also be able to advise you about precise equipment needs, and may also be able to suggest where to get it. But beware of being led into an expensive trap, and beware of being led into making someone else's video. You are the one in charge!

Negotiating

Be honest. If there is no money in it for them, say so at the outset. (You will, of course, be expected to pay for expenses like food, travel and lodging.) Avoid vague promises of future percentages of sales. If you are reasonably certain of future sales, and are prepared to fork out of your own pocket if they don't materialise, then put it in writing as a form of contract for their services. Otherwise you will be rumbled when the crew get to know you and your project better, and a resentful crew can be quite obstructive.

If you are relying on goodwill for help, be prepared for your chosen person no longer being available because they have been offered a paid job, and are not in a position to turn it down. Respect their decision – they may have a mortgage to pay and kids to feed. It's a good idea to ask them if they could recommend a colleague to step in.

If your budget enables you to pay a crew, it's better to go by whatever the local trade union rates and conditions are. You are more likely to be trusted by your crew. You should find out these rates in any case to avoid being overcharged! In the UK the relevant organisations are PACT (Producers Alliance for Cinema and Television) and BECTU (Broadcasting Entertainment Cinematograph and Theatre Union). See Useful Addresses and the budget section of Chapter 4.

Briefing

Obviously you should try and get copies of your script to everyone involved in helping you. In addition to this you should be able to discuss with the cameraperson what style of shooting you are after, e.g. carefully set up and beautifully lit scenes, or getting in close to fast-moving action. You may well be asked what your definition of a close up or wide shot is. This is quite variable and it saves time during shooting if that sort of thing is agreed upon in advance, if necessary with little sketches. If you are shooting on video with a monitor, it wastes time if you feel you have to play back every scene the cameraperson has just shot to check their framing agrees with your own ideas (you will also come across as questioning their ability), and if you are shooting on film you won't get the chance until you see your rushes, when it will be too late.

You should keep up your briefing throughout the shoot. You may be obliged by circumstances to change things in your script, and your crew will need to know. Making time in the schedule to see rushes at intervals during the shoot, whether shooting on film or tape, will enable you to fine tune your communication with the cameraperson and sound recordist.

Rembering the key points

1. Make sure you know their capabilities.

2. Be open about money.

3. Be open to suggestions, but stay in control.

4. Check local pay rates.

5. Communicate your intentions.

Case study: duping the crew

A would-be video producer, in the advertising business, wanted to make a video to sell holiday properties on an island in the Mediterranean. Knowing someone in the television business, he got together a crew of professionals (including the author, it has to be said) who were 'between jobs' with the lure of payment in Swiss francs – the crew would just be able to pocket it without the taxman knowing – and a 'free holiday for wives'.

He chartered a twelve-seater plane from the United Kingdom, and produced champagne on the flight. This aroused suspicions – the time for champagne is at the end of a successful shoot, not the beginning. Sure enough, towards the end of the week's shoot it became obvious that he didn't have the Swiss francs, and he had press-ganged the wives into babysitting for his own family. Please don't be one of these!

TAKING PICTURES

If someone is doing the camerawork for you, you won't need to read this section. But if you plan to do some or all of it yourself, and you have not done much videoing before, it will explain a few basic procedures. It's worth trying out various different kinds of lighting situations on a domestic camcorder, and playing them back on your television at home, to see what works and what doesn't, before embarking on an actual shoot. It always pays to read the instructions with a camcorder, or if you are hiring, and no instructions are included, get someone to show you over the equipment.

Setting the zoom

The zoom lens enables you to have wide angle, normal and telephoto lenses all in one. The so-called normal angle of view is that obtained when using a 35mm still camera with a 50mm lens on – no exaggerations or distortions to speak of – and approximates to normal human vision. The wider the angle of view the more you can include in the shot, but the perspectives will become emphasised, and things further away will appear very small. The narrower the angle of view the less will be included, and perspectives will be minimised, giving a 'crushed up' effect with objects further away being not much smaller than foreground ones.

The important thing to realise is that zooming in on a person, from a fixed camera position, does not have the same effect as moving the camera towards the person and leaving the zoom setting unchanged.

In both cases you go from a long shot, or wide angle view, of a person to a close up of their face. But in the first case, zooming in, you greatly reduce the amount of background in the shot, whereas in the second case, moving the camera nearer, the amount of background changes very little. The choice is yours!

Focusing

Many camcorders have automatic focusing, usually focusing on what is central in the frame. You may not want that, preferring to focus on a face on the edge of the frame, for instance. Or someone may walk through the shot (intentionally) in front of the person who is supposed to be sharp, and the camera will try to change the focus to the nearer person, and you probably won't want that to happen. So if you want to be able to control the focus, use a camcorder which has a manual focus option, and preferably one which has distance markings on the lens (check whether they are in feet or metres).

With a wide angle of view the difference in sharpness between a foreground person and the background is much less noticeable than it would be with a narrower, or telephoto, angle of view. So if you want to pick out a person as being sharply focused against a soft background you need to use the telephoto, or longer, end of the zoom. The effect will be increased in dimmer light where the lens aperture, which controls exposure, is likely to be 'wide open'.

Adjusting the exposure

Most camcorders have automatic exposure, that is to say they control
the opening of the lens aperture which determines how much light is
let in. If you want to control it yourself and prevent it from changing
in the middle of a shot, as would happen, for instance, if a white van
went through your picture, then use a camcorder with manual over-
ride, or a system for locking the exposure for the duration of the shot.
Some also have a 'variable shutter' – useful for shooting slow motion
effects with less blur on moving objects. But the faster the shutter
speed, the more light will be required to maintain correct exposure.

Film
Most film cameras will have manual exposure control only, via the
iris ring, so you will need to know about photography to get good
results. Your film laboratory will be able to give you reports the next
day on the exposure and general technical quality of your film rushes
during the shoot. It's always best to do some tests and have a talk
with them before you start shooting.

White balancing

This procedure ensures that your pictures are recorded with the correct colour balance whether using daylight or tungsten light, or strip
lighting. Domestic camcorders often have a white translucent cap
which you place over the lens, press a button, and the camcorder does
the rest. This won't be very effective in mixed lighting situations (see
above, Using light). If your camcorder has a white balance switch, a
better method is to point it at a piece of white card (it must be really
white) so that it fills most of the frame, and is positioned so that the
light falling on the card is a suitable mixture of the different light
sources you intend to use. Look at your colour monitor, with particular attention to flesh tones, and redo the white balance if you don't
like it with a different mix of light until you are happy.

Remember to reset the white balance when you return to a normal (unmixed) lighting situation.

Film
If you are shooting with tungsten-balanced film you need to use a
no. 85 conversion filter or equivalent for shooting in daylight. Using
a no. 81EF, a milder version of the no. 85, can give quite pleasing
results in mixed lighting such as dusk skylight mixed with tungsten
light bulbs. More subtle colour correction can be done at the print-
ing or transfer stage.

Using viewfinders and monitors

The viewfinder on a camcorder is usually just a small black and white monitor with an adjustable viewing lens in front of it, though some camcorders have a flip-up colour monitor on the side (if you use it, it will drain the battery faster). You therefore need to take note of what colours are in your shot. You can train your left eye to stay open to observe colours, and also see what's going on around you, while keeping the right eye to the viewfinder.

Alternatively you can use a colour monitor with a video lead from your camcorder. It will need to be powered either from mains or from battery, and in mobile situations it will slow you down. You can also use the colour monitor to check that the white balance the camcorder has chosen is giving you the results you want. But remember that to be meaningful the monitor must be correctly set up in the first place, so use the best quality monitor you can afford.

Film

If you are using a film camera you will be able to see full colour through the viewfinder, even without power, since you are actually looking through the lens via a mirrored shutter. This will give a flickering effect in the viewfinder when the camera is running. Remember to keep your eye to the viewfinder while filming. If you take your eye away stray light will get down the viewfinder and fog your image.

Checklist

Make sure you understand the following functions on your camcorder or film cameras:

- focusing
- exposure
- shutter speed (if applicable)
- white balancing.

SHOOTING INTERVIEWS

Interviews in one form or another seem to feature in most videos, particularly documentaries, and need to be conducted with care. There is a sense in which an interviewee gives a performance, like an actor. You as the questioner are having to 'direct an actor' who may be nervous (see Chapter 6). Part of your job is to put them at ease (unless you deliberately want to show up their nervousness), and part of your job is to go over immediately beforehand the ground you want to cover with them, partly to refresh their memory and partly to concentrate their mind so they don't become too verbose. But beware of letting them give their 'best performance' before you switch on the camera.

Asking questions

You will need to make a decision as to whether you want the questions to be heard, and therefore properly recorded, or whether you want the answers to stand on their own. You might even want the person asking the questions to be seen asking them. This is also a stylistic decision, since you will want to be consistent throughout your video about whether questions are heard or not.

If you intend not to use the questions, it might still be worth recording them so that when you come to the editing the editor will be more aware of what the interviewee is replying to. You will also have to explain to the interviewee that you want them to reply in such a way that the context of the question is included in their answer.

Example
Question: 'What was the most dangerous thing that happened to you while you were deep sea diving?'
Bad answer: 'A shark tried to bite through my airline. . .'
Even worse answer: 'Well now, I think it was when a shark tried . . . to bite through my airline. . .'
Good answers: 'The most dangerous thing that happened to me was when a shark. . .' or, 'The hairiest experience I ever had was when a shark. . .'

The good answer will stand on its own when you edit your video. The bad answer is like picking up the phone and coming in on the middle of a conversation with a crossed line. You will find that some interviewees are better than others at grasping this notion.

You will also need to watch out that the excitable interviewee doesn't start their answer before the questioner has finished speaking, otherwise it will cause problems when editing the sound track. In the recordist's terminology this is known as 'avoiding overlaps'.

Choosing eyelines

Where the interviewee looks will have a marked effect on the way they come across. The most usual set-up is for the questioner to sit or stand just to one side of the camera's lens. The interviewee looks at the questioner, and the viewer has the impression of the questioner being closely identified with the camera, since the interviewee's eyes are focused on a point very near the camera. The further away from the camera the interviewee looks, the less engaged they appear to be.

If you are intending to show the questioner as well, you will need to ensure that they and the interviewee have similar eyelines (see Respecting the 'line' on page 79). Unless you plan to use two cameras simultaneously, you will normally shoot their questions (rephrased if necessary) at the end of the interview, so someone needs to take a note of the questions during the interview. If, as sometimes happens, the interviewee is in a hurry to get away, you may need to put someone else in their place so that the questioner has someone to look at.

On some occasions you may want the interviewee, or person speaking, to look directly into the lens of the camera, so that the viewer has the impression that the speaker is addressing them directly. This can have a powerful effect if used sparingly. A well-known example of this is in the film *Richard the Third* where the actor Laurence Olivier makes occasional comments directly to the audience, thus involving them more closely in his plotting and scheming.

Autocue
This is a device for enabling someone to address the lens directly with a prepared statement which they will not be able to recite from memory. The text is projected across the front of the lens by means of an angled glass in such a way that the speaker can see it, but the camera, shooting from behind the glass, does not see it. It is expensive to hire and needs a skilled operator to work it. Avoid zooming in too close to the speaker's face, since the movement of their eyeballs as they scan the text will become more apparent, and detract from the effect of intimacy.

Selecting backgrounds
Backgrounds can tell the viewer a lot about the person being interviewed. The style of decor and type of furnishing, even if kept unobtrusively soft focus, will indicate the tastes, income level or interests of the interviewee. On the other hand, you may feel that that would detract from their identity as persons in their own right, particularly if what they are talking about doesn't relate in any way to their surroundings. The solution to that would be to ensure that the background is as plain and unobtrusive as possible, maybe even placing them in front of a black drape in a studio setting and lighting their features for maximum effect.

If there is an unavoidable noise in the background, such as trucks passing in the street, it can be less distracting for the viewer if a view of the street through a window is included in the background, so that the source of the noise is explained.

Lighting interviews

You should make sure that the lighting is comfortable for the interviewee. They should not be squinting in bright sunlight, or dazzled by too much front lighting in a room. The light from a window, or a 'recreated' window light, looks very natural and would generally be to one side. Backlights can help define the shape of a person's head, or add highlights in the hair, but are by no means always necessary, and might even look unnatural with a simple window light. They also tend to cause 'hot spots' on bald heads.

If you are in a studio setting it is sometimes worth putting some light on the questioner and what is behind him/her, even if you don't intend to shoot in that direction. This makes it more relaxing for the interviewee's eyes and takes away the feeling that they are being interrogated in a police cell.

Bear in mind also that lights tend to give out a lot of heat as well, and the sound recordist will probably want the windows and doors shut to exclude extraneous noise. So don't use more than you need, and leave time for taking a breather if it gets uncomfortably hot.

Using make up

Make up is normally a job for a specialist, but it's certainly worth having a powder puff handy to reduce the shine on a nose or a bald forehead.

Changing shot sizes

One way of shortening an interview in the editing is to be able to cut from a medium shot to a close shot, or vice versa. You could change the shot size on each question, but there is always the chance that if you reorder the interview in the editing you may still end up with two shots of the same size to be cut together. There is no foolproof method! You can also change shot size during an answer, particularly if you think you may want to cut out the middle of the speech later on, or if you want to go in closer for dramatic reasons.

You may also want to shoot a wider shot to reveal more of the setting of the interview, which can be used for putting commentary over to introduce the interviewee.

If you intend to use large parts of the interview as voice over other images, you may prefer to leave the shot size unchanged, since you are much less likely to need to cut together two separate sections of 'in vision' speech.

Shooting 'vox pops'

The name 'vox pop' (*vox populi* – voice of the people) derives from the time when television cameras first ventured onto the streets to ask random passers by their opinion on a topic. In general you would plan to use interviews of this sort as 'in vision' speech, since there is likely to be a good deal of background noise from traffic. They can be cut together later in rapid succession to show varying answers to the same question.

It's usually best to try and vary the background for each person, and to have the questioner first on one side of the camera then the other side, so that not everyone ends up looking in the same direction.

Remembering the key points

1. Make sure the interviewee is comfortable and feels at ease.

2. Make sure the replies will stand on their own if questions are not to be heard.

3. Think of how the interview will be edited later.

GETTING THE SHOTS YOU WANT

Remember that you are a video-maker, not a stills photographer. You have speech, sound effects and music to play with as well as images. So you need to think about such things as:

• How long will it take the viewer to 'read' the content or meaning of a shot?

• Is it necessary to establish the geography of a location?

• Will the lighting and colour match, or contrast with, the shot you intend to follow or precede?

• Would a simpler, plainer shot be less distracting if important speech is to go over it later in the editing?

These are aesthetic considerations which can become quite complex. So to avoid mental paralysis setting in during the shoot, do the thinking beforehand, and then stick to keeping it simple and trusting your instincts.

Low angles
You can make effective use of low angle shots for conveying ideas like 'a child's eye view of authority'. Small tripods known as 'baby legs' can be used for this, or the camera can be propped up on the ground with wedges to steady it if you don't need to pan or tilt it.

High angles
Looking down on a subject, from the roof of a building or a balcony, can give a feeling of detachment, or even omnipotence. Or it can serve a more mundane purpose like establishing the geography of a place, or giving a sense of space to a flat landscape. A length of rope sometimes comes in handy for hoisting equipment up ladders and through small hatches in church towers.

Respecting the 'line'
There is a certain line which you cross at your peril! Imagine you are shooting a football game from the sidelines. Your shots will cut together without confusion if you stay on the same side of the pitch. But if you take shots from the other side as well there will be confusion in the mind of the viewer about which team is playing in which direction when you cut them in with shots from the first side. There is a 'line' down the middle of the pitch.

The same applies to a conversation between two people. Shots of each of them will cut together if taken from the same side of an imaginary line between them. But if you cross the line one of them will appear to be looking in the wrong direction when you cut them together.

Tracking
Moving the camera sideways can impart a sense of depth to a scene, when near and far objects appear to move in relation to one another as you track the camera. A more obvious use is to follow a person as they move.

Example: filming a dance on stage
If you were to film a pas de deux dance sequence on a stage from a fixed position in the front stalls, you would see into the wings everytime you panned the camera left or right to follow the dancers. If you are able to track along the front of the stage you would be able to

keep the backcloth scenery behind them as you followed them across the stage.

Before planning an elaborate and time-consuming tracking shot, you should ask yourself whether you will actually be able to use it in the editing. The sequence may end up too long, and half a day's shooting goes out the window!

Hand holding

The latest camcorders have become so small and light that there is a temptation to hand hold everything and dispense with a tripod. But a lighter camera is really harder to hold steady than a heavier one. Shots where the camera is static (or meant to be), such as landscapes, buildings or static interviews, should be done with a tripod. There will always be some wavering about which will be distracting if you try and hand hold the camera. But if you are in a crowded or mobile situation, or you want to make a deliberate and positive move with the camera, then hand holding can be the answer.

Small camcorders with flip-up auxiliary monitors, or large viewfinders, are particularly useful because you can move the camera through a quite complicated path without having to keep your eye up to the viewfinder, and still see what you are getting.

Listening

If you are shooting an interview or a group discussion, develop the habit of listening to the flow of the talk. You will soon be able to sense whether a person is about to stop talking, or move on to a new point, which could be an opportunity to change the size of the shot. Having a choice of sizes in an interview gives the editor more options when cutting it down to length.

You may also be able to sense who is going to talk next in a group discussion. Remember that your sound recordist will follow the talk with the microphone, but you have the option of getting the facial reactions of those not talking. Listening to the flow will help you decide when to pan the camera. Once you make a decision, follow it through as a definite move. Hesitations in the camerawork will be a nightmare for the editor.

Getting cutaways

The cutaway has become a conventional means of bridging a time gap in a sequence, often an interview, so as to avoid a 'jump' cut. They work best if they are relevant to what is being said, otherwise they seem like mechanical aids for editing, where you might just as well use a short dissolve or a second of blank screen.

If you are shooting an interview and you know you will need to edit it down to length, have a good look around the room to see if there are any relevant objects, such as family photos, which you could shoot afterwards as cutaways.

Shooting aerials

Don't automatically assume you will need a helicopter. These are very expensive to hire, and rigging the camera and checking for safety will take up a lot of time. Simple 'bird's eye view' shots of landscape can be done from a two-seater top wing aircraft, such as a tiger moth, for a fraction of the cost, by pushing up the window flap by the passenger seat and shooting through the forty-five degree gap between the wing strut and the landing wheel.

The secret of any aerial shooting, whether helicopter or tiger moth, is in having a good, well-briefed pilot who understands where you want the lens to point, *and* who will not take risks.

Rostrum work

If you plan to use still photographs, paintings or other static art work, you can shoot these yourself by rigging up a suitable board and system for attaching the art work such as blue tack or rubber bands. Two lights either side at forty-five degrees or more will give an even light, but you will need to take care to avoid flaring with shiny photographs.

If you have a good tripod with a smooth working pan and tilt you can even do simple moves. For more complicated work you will need to use the services of a professional rostrum camera company (see Production Manuals, listed in the Useful Addresses section).

Make your shots meaningful in the context of your project, not just pretty pictures. To achieve this make sure your camera-person understands your intentions.

8
Editing It

INTRODUCTION

Hopefully you will have given thought to the editing before shooting began. You will have selected an editor, unless you aim to do your own editing, and you will have at least provisionally booked the facilities. You will have discussed with the editor such practical matters as logging, slating and time code, as well as the creative aspects. Following the editor's requirements during shooting can save a lot of time and money when it comes to the editing.

If your shooting schedule involves shooting over a period of time, with gaps in between sessions, you can start editing as soon as enough material has been shot for an editor to get their teeth into. Furthermore, any potential problems in the method or style of shooting can be spotted early on by the editor, so that the rest of your shooting can incorporate their suggestions.

EDITING TECHNIQUES

Your editing, or 'cutting' as it is sometimes known as, will usually involve more than simply shortening a sequence. Here are some basic techniques:

- continuity
- parallel action
- sound overlays
- montage.

Example: recording a wedding
You have shot the bride preparing herself at her house, you have shot the bridegroom with his friends, then the ceremony, followed by the reception and the couple driving off. Now you need to edit your material down to a suitable length. In **continuity** editing you follow the order of events, making sure that your shots flow smoothly. You might

omit, for instance, some shots of the groom arriving first at the church if it was not important to see the church at this point.

Alternatively you might decide to show the bride's preparations and the groom journeying with his friends simultaneously with **parallel action**. After a few shots of the bride, you show the groom, and then back to the bride at a later stage, and so on. This is not only a way of shortening the material, it can also create more of a sense of expectation in the audience. Will he or she get there on time?

Think also of what you could do with the **sound** track. After shots of the bride's preparations, continue the sound of the bride and her bridesmaids chattering over shots of the groom waiting in the church. This might raise a laugh – or it might not! Later in the editing you could think about using additional sounds over the images, such as music, or narration by the bride's father.

Another possibility might be to create a **montage** for the beginning or end of the video. Short shots of the bride, the ring being put on, the cake being cut, confetti being thrown – building up a sequence which is almost like a commercial for a wedding

Structuring ideas

If your project is more about ideas and concepts than about covering an event, you will need to think about how to contrast opposing views, or how to dramatically build up a convincing argument. Where you place a particularly strong statement or interview will affect the dramatic balance of your video. The sound from such an interview could be layed over complementary images, or over contrasting ones, reinforcing the statement or questioning it.

Example: environmentally unfriendly

An oil company executive is speaking about his company's environmentally friendly products and policies. You could lay the sound over a complementary sequence of shots showing their installations in a sunny landscape with lots of trees, happy couples filling up at a garage, smiling cyclists riding down country lanes, and so on. Or, you could lay it over a contrasting sequence of shots showing leaking tankers fouling the sea, a haze of exhaust fumes over a crowded motorway, cyclists in a big city wearing breathing masks, and so on, where the message *you* are conveying is very different from what the executive is saying. (Be prepared for a lawsuit!)

Remembering the key points

1. Your material can have a very different impact by being reordered, by overlaying sounds on other images, or by strategically using voice over to reinforce, or question, an image.

2. Editing can be a very creative process, but requires careful judgement about how a particular technique is likely to affect your audience. It's easy to get carried away and end up making a satire.

3. Finally, allow time for thinking. It would be a pity not to allow sufficient editing time in your budget to take full advantage of the possibilities in your shot material.

EDITING SYSTEMS

The advent of computer technology has brought about the concept of **linear** and **non-linear** editing. These terms have become common in editing parlance, as have the terms **off line** and **on line**.

Editing with linear systems

You edit, or make a cut, by re-recording the chosen scenes in their new order onto a fresh, specially prepared tape. Since the tape cannot be physically cut, any alterations or additions to a particular cut will mean re-recording onto a new prepared tape in order to preserve the subsequent edits. This will involve a generation loss from the alteration point onward, the tedious alternative being to re-do all the edits subsequent to the alteration.

Using non-linear systems

These make use of disk storage technology. The visual and audio material which you have shot is loaded into the system's memory digitally. You can then access the material in any order and any number of times. This means you can change an edit without the loss of quality from further generations associated with linear systems. It is similar to a word processor, enabling the user to insert new paragraphs without having to retype all subsequent text. **Avid** and **Lightworks** are current examples of this type of equipment.

Some of the recent small digital camcorders can be connected directly to a personal computer, and a television set, to enable you to perform simple editing functions.

Working off line

This is more a mode of operation than a specific piece of machinery. Editing 'off line' simply means doing your edits with lots of trial and error, trying out different editing ideas, without actually finishing with a completed master edit. Where quality loss from re-doing edits is not important, you can use linear tape systems in this mode.

However, non-linear systems are increasingly being used in the off-line mode. They are much faster at finding the required scenes to edit (rather like searching on a compact disc), and because they are digital there is no loss of quality when making changes. When you were writing your script on a word processor and making lots of alterations, you were editing words off line with a non-linear system.

Going on line

Editing systems used in the on-line mode produce a final edited master from the original tapes. Thus a basic linear tape editing system could be used on line if you are happy to accept a certain loss of quality due to having to go through one or more generations of re-recording. Likewise a non-linear system such as **Avid** can be used in an on-line mode if it is to record onto a master tape after having achieved a satisfactory edit off line, provided it is hooked up to the appropriate tape recording machinery. Similarly your script went 'on line' when you instructed your word processor to make a print out.

In addition, on-line systems have the ability to incorporate additional sound tracks, special editing effects such as wipes or multi images, and complex sound mixes not possible with the off-line system.

Creating an EDL (edit decision list)

Professional editing systems designed to be used on line have the ability to receive instructions in the form of EDLs from off-line machines.

If you write out on a piece of paper the time code numbers at the entry and exit points of each shot, in order from beginning to end, of your completed off-line edit, you will have an EDL. Remember, the time code numbers (see Chapter 7) were either originated in your camcorder during shooting, or were put on afterwards before editing started. Shots are selected from the tape originals, via the time code references, in the order of the edit set out in the EDL, and are recorded onto a new master tape.

Most professional off-line editing suites can print out an EDL. You can then take it to your on-line edit suite as a foolproof set of instructions for your final on-line edit, even if you do it a year later and have forgotten the editing decisions you made.

Film
Film was in use before the new terminology came into being, so it is less easy to classify. Editing on film is off line in the sense that a work print, or cutting copy, is made from the original negative. You can then edit the work print in a cutting room equipped with a machine for viewing sections of film and a means of assembling the edited sections together onto a reel.

It is also non-linear in the sense that there is random access to material during the off-line stage, and alterations can be inserted into an edited workprint without having to re-copy scenes, or re-edit everything, subsequent to the alteration. You simply wind down the reel to the required point, get out the scissors, and insert the new section of film, usually with selotape joins which can be undone again if necessary.

You go 'on line' when you cut the original negative to match the work print. This is done using a set of numbers, called **key numbers** ('keykode' is the Kodak trade name), which are printed through onto the workprint from the negative, where they were put on by the manufacturer, allowing for frame accurate negative cutting.

Remembering the key points

1. Off-lining is rehearsing, on-lining is the actual performance.

2. Non-linear systems, although more expensive, are more convenient to use than linear systems, and they save time.

3. Editing on film can be thought of as non-linear, and the machinery is not expensive.

CHOOSING AN EDITING SYSTEM

What route you choose for your editing will depend on the following factors:

1. **Budget.** Professional non-linear edit suites are relatively expensive to hire, although you can save money by avoiding the plush suites which offer leather sofas, constant coffee and other distractions. If you only need to distribute a small number of copies for home viewing and you don't need any complex effects, you can do trial edits, in an off-line mode, and then edit on line, with a simple two-machine editing set-up on VHS.

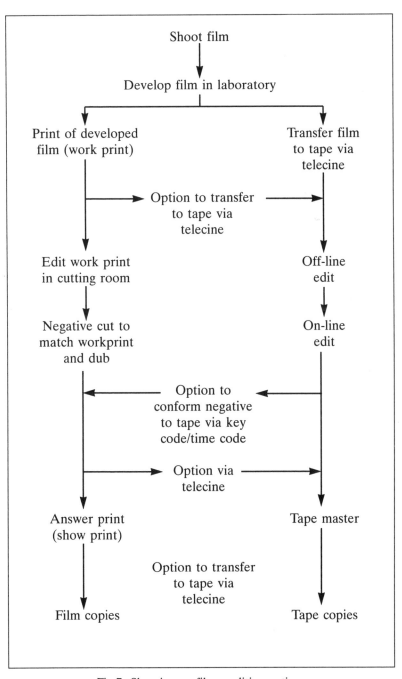

Fig 7. Shooting on film – editing options.

2. **Time available.** If time is short it might work out no more expensive to use a non-linear system for speed and convenience, rather than a cheaper but slower linear system.

3. **Outlet.** If you are aiming at broadcast quality, even if you shot on HI-8, you will need to 'bump up' to a broadcast quality format, usually Beta SP, and use a non-linear digitised system such as Avid. Even if it is not for broadcast but you aim for a high volume distribution, it is worth on-lining to Beta SP to maintain the best possible image quality in the copies.

4. **Access to free or subsidised facilities**. If you are getting help from a workshop for instance you would want to use their editing facilities, though they might not be equipped with the latest non-linear digital suites.

5. **Capacity.** If you have a large amount of material to edit, the result of a very high shooting ratio, you may find that the capacity of the non-linear system you had your eye on is not sufficient to store your material. You would then have to do a pre-edit on a linear system in order to reduce your material to what the equipment can handle.

Film
If you have shot on film you will have a choice of editing on film, or transferring your developed negative to a master tape (Beta SP or equivalent quality) and then doing your off-line edit on a non-linear system, loading your master tape into its memory, or using VHS copy tapes with burnt in timecode to off-line on a cheaper system.

Once you have done your on-line edit, you will have a new master tape of your final version for making distribution copies. Your original camera negative will remain untouched, with possible archival value, or the possibility of making a new programme in the future with a high quality film original which will be compatible with any new video system of the future, not yet invented.

If you are aiming at cinema showings you will need to cut your original negative ('on line') to make cinema prints. If you are *only* exhibiting in cinemas then it would make sense to edit on film, leaving out tape altogether. Otherwise, if you want to have tape distribution as well, you can edit on tape, on-lining on tape and film (negative cutting), or edit on film and make a tape transfer from your cinema print. The flow chart in Figure 7 will give you an indication of your main options.

The possible permutations of juggling between film and tape are many and can be expensive, and constitute a technical and budgetary minefield for the unwary. So if you are going down this route you will need careful budgeting, and expert advice from your editor.

Remembering the key points

1. Linear off-line suites are cheap to hire.

2. Non-linear off-line suites are faster to use but are generally more expensive to use per hour/day.

3. On-line suites are seriously expensive and should only be used when all possible editing decisions have already been made in the off-line mode.

4. Film editing is 'non-linear', but definitely 'hands on' and relatively cheap per hour/day.

CHOOSING AN EDITOR

The same considerations apply to choosing your editor as to choosing a crew (see Chapter 7), but you should also bear in mind that editors vary in their talents. There are those who are highly skilled in operating the complex machinery of an on-line edit suite, but who may not have much to suggest in the way of creative input, and then there are those who make brilliant creative suggestions for solving apparently intractable problems, but who may be slow at operating on-line machinery.

The first kind will save you money in the on-line suite because they are quick, but they may be just a 'yes' person. If your project does not require any complex editing, then your best choice might be to go straight into an on-line suite, armed with all the details of your handwritten EDL, and leave it to an efficient on-line editor.

However, if your project is going to involve difficult editing decisions, then you should find a good off-line editor who will be sympathetic to your subject, and able to make creative editing suggestions based on their own perceptions of your material. You, however, must remain in charge. Be open to suggestions, but at the end of the day it will be your decision. They will be able to take you right up to the on-line stage with a completed edit, except for any fancy effects and sound mixes that can only be done with the on-line facilities, and can accompany you in the on-line suite to supervise the on-line editor.

If you are lucky you may be able to find all these talents in one editor.

Remembering the key points

1. Look for someone with good creative input if your project is complex.

2. Be prepared to use two editors, one off-line and one on-line.

DIGESTING YOUR MATERIAL

Before you, or your editor, start the actual business of editing, you should make time to review all the material which you have shot, and also if possible any archive material you may be planning to use. Even better if you can take a few days break after the end of shooting, so that you can take a more critical attitude towards it.

What you have shot will be what you have to make your video with. Before shooting began you hammered out a script to work from. Now you have to ask yourself, 'Does the material I have shot match up with the script?' Other questions you might ask yourself are:

- Have my perceptions about the subject changed as a result of the shooting experience?

- Does that interviewee come over on video the way I thought they did at the time?

- Have I succeeded in capturing that sense of geographical space I was hoping for?

- Has the brief changed?

- Has the sponsor (if there is one) still got the same expectations?

- Or (more alarming!) am I still dealing with the same person?

- Has the political (in the broadest sense) situation changed since shooting began?

Transferring from the original

To review your material, you will need to get it transferred to VHS copies which you can view at home, on an ordinary domestic VCR (video cassette recorder). Playing your original camcorder tapes, even if you originally shot on the standard VHS format, is not advisable. You risk damaging them and causing 'drop out', those white lines and blobs which appear on a damaged tape.

You should ask for time code to be 'burnt in' so that it becomes visible in the picture area. If you shot without professional time code, on a HI-8 camcorder for example, or an older film camera, time code will be put on when your original tapes, or developed negative, are transferred to a new high quality format (usually Beta SP), and your VHS viewing copies from this will have the time code burnt in.

Checklist
• Make sure the transfer facility understand what tape format or digital system you will be using for your editing.

• Ask for time code to be burnt in on your viewing tapes.

Viewing rushes
You are now in a position to look for answers to those questions you posed earlier. It might even be helpful to have someone else, whose opinion you value, view some or all of it with you. Keep notes about all your impressions. They will be useful to refer to later to compare with the perhaps more jaded impressions you may have later on in your editing.

Making transcripts
You should have typed transcripts made of all interview material and distribute copies to the editor, and anyone else interested. If you recorded the interviews on a separate audio cassette at the time of shooting (many sound recordists offer this facility), then transcripts can be made from the audio cassettes while you are viewing your material, or even during your shooting.

Making a paper edit
With any project involving interviews or long speeches needing to be cut in length, it is worthwhile to do a preliminary 'paper edit' by cutting out required paragraphs from the typed transcript and pasting them together in your selected order, with notes of the time code (from your viewing tapes) at the beginning and end of each section.

Paper edits can save a lot of time, and therefore money, later in the edit suite, and give the editor something to start on. Even if your project is a simple one, it will still be useful for the editor to have a list of time code references in your selected order, particularly if you shot the material out of sequence.

Remembering the key points

1. Note down time code references for the beginning and end of selected sections.

2. Be prepared to depart from your original script if the material dictates it.

SHAPING YOUR MATERIAL

Having viewed your rushes and worked out on paper how you are going to assemble your material, you can now go into the off-line suite and start putting together your first assembly.

If you are going to edit your own material you can look forward to long hours of staring at monitors and searching for scenes. Your time code log will help you to find your shots. If it's a linear off-line suite, time will be spent rewinding tapes and inserting new ones, particularly when your edit order is very different from the order in which you shot your material. In a non-linear suite, finding shots will be quicker, since all your material will have been loaded into the machine's memory.

Unless you are already very familiar with operating the editing machinery, this is where you will start wishing you had an editor to work with you. Let us assume, therefore, that you have booked an editor.

Working with the editor

Your presence at this stage is not strictly necessary, since if your paper edit is sufficiently detailed and clear, the editor should be able to construct the first assembly from it on their own. Yet you may well wish to observe the editor's reactions to certain scenes, or to structural decisions you have made, and to assess whether they have grasped the intentions behind your project. Being shut away all day in an edit suite can be a lonely business, and mutual encouragement can make things easier. On the other hand, some editors prefer to work alone, uninterrupted, once they have been briefed, until they are ready to show you an assembly.

Viewing the first assembly

Expect to be depressed! It will almost certainly be too long, and there are bound to be ideas which turn out not to work as you had hoped. But at least you can now see it as a whole.

You will probably need to view it more than once. If a sponsor is involved it's usually better not to let them see the first assembly. Your editor will be able to give you their impression and make suggestions about possibly reordering sequences, or using parts of an interview as voice over other images.

It will also become apparent to you what points will need to be reinforced by commentary. Any weaknesses in your original script will show up at this stage.

Checklist
- Do I have a beginning, a middle and an end?

- Have I got the right balance between explanatory and dramatic material?

- Have I got the right balance between interviews expressing contrasting views?

- Is the pacing right?

- At what points am I likely to need music?

Editing on film
If you have shot on film and you intend to edit on film rather than transfer your developed negative to tape (see flow chart, Figure 7), then you will order a print of all your material from the laboratory, and transfers of all your sound tapes onto sprocketed magnetic film. Your 'off-line edit suite' will be a film cutting room equipped with rewinding benches, a Steenbeck or similar machine for viewing reels of film with sound, a cutting and joining device known as a splicer, and bins with racks for hanging up selected lengths of film.

Synchronising sound and picture
Before you sit down to digest your material, your editor will need to assemble your picture and sound on separate reels so that in each scene the sound is synchronised with the picture. If you shot with time code he/she will be able to do this by matching the time code numbers printed through onto picture and sound. Otherwise they will synchronise sound and picture with the traditional clapper board used at the front or end of each shot, and will have a set of numbers, known as **rubber numbers**, printed on the edges of picture and sound to ensure they can always be matched up again even when cut into pieces.

Viewing rushes

If you can afford it, you can have a VHS tape transfer made of all your synchronised material which you can then view at home at your leisure. All the slate numbers will be visible on the clapper boards, so you can make notes to build up a paper edit, and if you shot with time code you can have it burnt in.

Otherwise you will have to view your material in the cutting room, or projected onto a screen – which will give you the opportunity to fine check things like focus. This can also be an occasion for the editor to get familiar with the material.

Then you can proceed with your first assembly, as you would with tape.

FURTHER CUTTING

Once you have considered your first assembly, you can move towards your rough cut, doing more detailed editing of individual sequences, perhaps using some of the techniques outlined at the beginning of this chapter. Some points to bear in mind at this stage are:

• Keep notes of alternative shot orders which you may have rejected for the moment.

• Keep a note of the duration of each sequence.

• Leave cuts in an interview as 'jump' cuts for the time being – it's the sound that matters at this stage. Cutaways can go in later.

Weighing your shots

It is easy to become over-familiar with your material through constant viewing in the edit suite, and to forget how a shot might strike an audience on a first viewing. You need to 'weigh' it in the sense of assessing how long it will take to register with the viewer. This will depend on its composition and lighting as well as the content.

Example: tigers and deer

A close shot of a snarling tiger can be held for a very short time since its impact is strong and immediate, whereas a long shot of a tiger half hidden in long grass stalking a deer drinking at a lake contains quite a lot of information, both visually and as narrative, and would need to be held for a longer time.

For this reason it is usually better to cut visual sequences purely on their visual 'weight' before fitting music, rather than to cut shots to the beat of an already chosen piece of music.

Summary

Digest your material and do a paper edit before starting on the off-line stage. Then assess your first assembly, try alternate versions, and do further editing. You follow the same thought processes whether editing on tape or film.

WRITING YOUR COMMENTARY

Commentary, or 'narration' as it is also known, can fulfil several functions:

- adding information not already in the sound or visuals

- expressing an opinion on what is seen

- narrating a parallel story

- revealing a character's inner thoughts or feelings.

Of course, you may not need any commentary if you think what you have shot is self-explanatory when edited. But this is very difficult to achieve, even with the most thorough scripting and planning.

Before you write any commentary you must know how much space there is for it. You will need to measure the duration of the relevant sequence, then, as a rule of thumb, assume you only have half that time for commentary.

Keeping the audience's attention

Remember that the eye takes precedence over the ear, as far as your viewers are concerned. If your commentary is filling in with facts and figures, very little of it will be retained by the viewers if at the same time they are watching an exciting visual event on the screen. Overloading your video with statistics will turn them off.

If the information is important you can always offer it separately as a leaflet once the audience is hooked (cf. pamphlets and books offered by Channel Four and BBC after airing certain documentaries).

Recording the commentary

You can do this anywhere so long as there is no background noise – in the living room at three o'clock in the morning, for example. Some edit suites will incorporate a soundproof booth for this purpose. The commentator will need to work to your accurate timings, perhaps rehearsing to check that their delivery will fit your timings. This can be made easier if you can arrange for them to see the sequence on a monitor as they record.

Unless you are recording 'live' at the on-line edit, it's worth recording several takes of each section of commentary if there is any doubt about precise timings, or to have alternative voice inflexions.

Make sure that the tape format you record onto is compatible with the editing system you are using, and that there is an appropriate time code.

Remembering the key points

1. Be sparing with commentary.

2. Be clear what you want it to do.

3. Make accurate timings.

4. Record it with absolutely no background noise.

USING MUSIC

Some possible uses of music might be:

- to help establish a mood

- to identify a recurring character or situation (a 'leitmotif' in musical terminology)

- to blend together apparently random images

- to replace naturalistic sound effects, thereby intensifying the effect of the images

- to use with titles at the front and end of your video.

In general you will not want the music to attract too much attention to itself, except where you use it as a kind of fanfare to announce something.

You should also think seriously about whether you actually need music. Many effective videos are made without it, and you should not rely on it as a means of propping up a weak script.

Finding music

You have three choices:

1. You can choose a piece of existing music you know would work well for your project. But you will need copyright clearance (see Chapter 9).

2. You can go to a music library (see Useful Addresses) and select appropriate music from various categories headed 'dramatic', 'peaceful', 'military', and so on.

3. You can commission music to be specially written for your video.

If you plan to use already existing music, or music from a library, you will need to arrange for a transfer to the tape format you require.

Getting music composed

The composer will need to have accurate timings for each section of music you intend to use. You should also arrange for them to view your rough cut so that they can get a feeling for what you want.

You are unlikely to have the budget for a full orchestra, so it's best to think in terms of one or two instruments. Some composers use electronic systems which can reproduce the flavour of a variety of different conventional instruments. These devices, similar to word processors, also dish up a recording on audio tape, saving the business of organising a recording session to record the performance of the music.

Get the composer to play over to you the main themes in order to satisfy yourself that they are on the right track.

Recording music

As with commentary, you must record music where there is absolutely no background noise, preferably in a music recording studio with specially designed acoustics. The composer will generally find the players. In the case of a music video, you will, of course, record the music before shooting the pictures with a music playback system.

You will need to ensure that you end up with a tape format compatible with the editing system you are using.

Remembering the key points

1. Be clear what you want the music to do.

2. Make sure it's available to you in the right format.

3. Specially composed music can be a cheap and effective option.

VIEWING YOUR ROUGH CUT

Your important editing decisions have been carried out, commentary written, and music selected. You and your colleagues can now assess it.

Getting approval

At this stage (still off line) you may also wish to bring in a sponsor or client in order to get their approval as to content. You may need to read the commentary yourself if it's not possible to incorporate it on the sound track before on-lining, and to explain that, with linear off-lining, picture quality will not be as it will be when on-lined. Music, graphics and other effects may also be missing.

It is particularly important that you get approval for any technical procedures which are shown in your video, because once you have done your on-line edit it is likely to be a very expensive business to make alterations.

If the overall shape and message of your video is still not working to everyone's satisfaction, then take a break and start again. Don't assume that some magical solution to the problem will present itself at the online edit.

ON-LINING

You have reached the point where you have made your structural decisions, you have written the commentary and chosen the music. It remains to tidy up loose ends, so that everything flows smoothly when you get to the on-line suite.

Checklist

1. Check all your visual cuts to make sure there are no awkward jumps in action.

2. Check that the ins and outs of interview cuts are clean and sound natural. Cutting points may make sense on paper, but don't always sound natural.

3. Check that your commentary fits easily over the intended sequence. It's usually more effective to allow the sequence to

establish itself before bringing in the commentary, otherwise it will sound rushed and the audience will feel a conflict between picture and sound.

4. Check that your music fits, and that it will come in and go out at the beginning or end of a musical phrase. Check also that commentary and music are staggered, and do not start or stop together.

5. Check that you have copyright clearances (see Chapter 9). Finding out *after* on-lining that you can't afford to use that piece of music will cost you dear.

6. Check that the overall length is what it should be. If it's for television a very precise length will be stipulated, and there may have to be 'break' points for advertisements.

7. Finally check that you have everything to hand for the on-line edit:

   - all your original material
   - any archive material you may be using
   - any graphics or still photographs
   - titles, including any subtitling
   - commentary
   - music and any special sound effects
   - your EDL (edit decision list).

You will now be able to create a new master tape incorporating not only all the edit decisions you made in the off-line suite, but also all the features which were not possible off line, such as dissolves, wipes, multi-imaging, and any other special effects available in the on-line suite you are using.

There will also be the opportunity to correct colour balance on scenes which need it.

If the suite has a video rostrum camera (most do), you will be able to feed in prepared art work, photographs, and so on. The video camera will be set up to simply record the image straight onto your new master tape.

Mixing the sound
You will be able to create a fully mixed sound track, with all the music and commentary added, and any variations in background noise levels in edited interviews will be ironed out.

Foreign versions

You also have the opportunity of making a separate 'music and effects' track which you can use at a later date to make versions with commentary in a foreign language.

Warning!

If you are unfamiliar with the sometimes claustrophobic atmosphere of an on-line edit suite, you may become visually confused about exactly what is going on. There will be a number of monitors, showing outgoing and incoming scenes, and you might even lose track of whether a shot is playing forwards or backwards. Before starting, it's worth asking the on-line editor to point out to you what each monitor is showing.

Checking as you go

Make sure that each cut or short sequence works to your satisfaction. If necessary ask the editor to replay that section. Remember that you are recording on to a new tape and are actually working in a *linear* mode (unless you can afford the luxury of a non-linear on-line suite, and they are increasingly on offer).

Remembering the key points

1. Have everything prepared before going to the on line suite.

2. Check each section as you go along.

Preparing film for on-lining

Mostly the same points apply as in preparing to on line with tape, except that titles, graphics, and so on are included at the off-line stage. You will need to shoot them on film and cut them into your edit along with your other material.

Track laying

You can lay several different sound tracks all in synchronisation with the picture, each wound onto its own reel, a process known as 'track laying'. This gives you the chance of trying out overlapping sounds on separate tracks, such as commentary coming in under music, ready for mixing at the on line.

Normally all dialogue, whether interviewees or actors, is layed over two tracks, alternating on each cut, enabling differences in background noise between cut sections to be ironed out in the mixing.

Sound effects, commentary and music will each have a separate track.

On-lining with film

The main difference from tape is that you start by creating the sound track in a re-recording studio, sometimes known as a 'dubbing theatre', mixing all your pre-layed tracks as you view the same workprint you worked on in the cutting room. You need to check that the sound is working to your satisfaction as you go along since, as with tape, you are in a linear mode.

Negative cutting

You now have a completed sound track, but still only a scratched and dirty work print for the visuals. The next stage is to cut your original negative to match the work print, using the 'key numbers' printed through from the negative (see page 86). You should get a professional 'neg cutter' to do this, in super hygienic conditions. Your film laboratory (see Useful Addresses) may offer this service, or there are facilities companies offering negative cutting, along with synchronisation of rushes, transcripts and so on.

Making copies

Once your negative has been cut you can ask the laboratory to make a trial print, known as an **answer print**, for your approval as to contrast and colour quality. Your cameraperson should be able to help you with this. When that is satisfactory you can order subsequent prints with sound for distribution and exhibition as film, or make a transfer to a master tape on any format or standard that is required, anywhere in the world.

Alternatively you can transfer your cut negative straight to a master tape, eliminating the print stage, and then make distribution tape copies from the master tape. If you later decide you want a print, for a film festival for example, you still have your cut negative stored in readiness. (See Figure 7.)

Remembering the key points

1. Get the sound mix right before cutting the negative to match the workprint.

2. Make sure your negative is handled professionally in clean surroundings.

9
Dealing with Copyright

CONTACTING THE RIGHT ORGANISATIONS

In most cases you will need to contact the **MCPS (Mechanical Copyright Protection Society).** *Address*: Elgar House, 41 Streatham High Road, London SW16 1ER. Tel: (0181) 664 4400. Fax: (0181) 769 8792.

Already existing music
Music written by a composer who has been dead for more than seventy years is in the 'public domain' and no permission is needed. All other music, including by the way the tune *Happy Birthday To You*, is in copyright. A *recording* of a work made in the last fifty years will have a separate copyright which must also be cleared. You would still need clearances, for example, even if you want to use a part of an HMV (His Master's Voice) recording of Beethoven's *Ninth Symphony* made in 1975. Similarly you will also need clearance if someone in your video plays *Happy Birthday* on the piano.

If your video is to be for sale or hire, you will have to pay royalties based on the duration of the music you use, and the number of videos sold or hired, on an ongoing basis. Even if it is not for sale, it is still a legal requirement to obtain copyright clearance.

Libraries
If you plan to use music from a library (known as Production Music Libraries – see Useful Addresses) you will simply pay a standard rate based on thirty-second units with copyright clearances included as part of the package, and you will be asked to sign a code of conduct.

Specially composed music
You will need to draw up a contract with the composer, and the terms of the contract will determine whether copyright will reside with you or the composer, so you won't need to contact the MCPS, unless you want advice.

Public performances

A television or cable showing of your video would constitute a public performance of the music in it. Copyright clearance and royalties for public performance of music is handled by a different organisation, the **PRS (Performing Right Society)**. *Address*: 29–33 Berners Street, London, W1P 4AA . Tel: (0171) 580 5544. Fax: (0171) 631 4138.

It is normally the television or cable company who will deal with the PRS, since they are responsible for the public performance, but you will still need to inform the television company of the copyright and royalties situation for any music in your video.

GETTING CLEARANCE

When you have decided on the already existing music you plan to use, you should have the following information available for the MCPS.

Music details
- title
- composer
- performer
- publisher
- record company (if relevant)
- duration of music
- context of use/arrangements

Production details
- production title (title of your project)
- production company (you, if you are not a company)
- client (if applicable)
- format of production (tape, film, or whatever comes along in the future)
- number of copies
- territory of distribution
- subject matter, or synopsis of your video

The rates you may have to pay will depend on the duration of the music you use, how wide a territory your distribution will cover (United Kingdom only will be cheaper than world-wide), and the 'price' of the particular music you have chosen. If your video is a fundraising appeal for a charity you may be able to negotiate free use.

Summary

1. Using library music is a simple 'package deal' procedure.

2. Using already composed and/or recorded music will involve copyright clearances with the MCPS.

3. If using specially composed music make sure the copyright ownership is made clear.

10
Launching your Video

STAGING A PRESENTATION

There are several reasons for having a presentation including:

1. To help get publicity for your video.

2. To get feedback and comments.

3. As a thank you for those involved in helping you make it.

Getting publicity
To get your video talked about you will need to:

• Invite people whom you know would have an interest in seeing your video, and who might pass the word around their colleagues.

• Invite representatives from any relevant trade press or journal.

• If your video is to be for sale, invite representatives from any relevant video distributor or hire company, or bookseller who deals in videos as well (see Useful Addresses).

• Have an introductory brochure to hand out, giving brief details of what your video is about, that guests can take away with them. If you can afford it, include one or two still photographs from your video. This will mean finding time to take some good quality still photographs at key points during your shooting.

Getting feedback
Most people would be unwilling to tell you to your face that they don't like your video. But if you value opinions about the effectiveness or usefulness of your video, you could hand out questionnaires with self-addressed stamped envelopes, asking:

• Did the video arouse your interest?

- Did it make you want to find out more?

- Was it the right length?

- Was it relevant to you and why?

- Was it easy to assimilate?

- What would you have liked to see that you didn't see?

- Was the technical quality up to your expectations?

If you can get people to answer these sort of questions it will be more valuable to you than simply asking them to fill in a score sheet, where they tick boxes numbered one to five to give good and bad ratings.

ARRANGING VIEWING FACILITIES

Small groups

You will naturally want your first showing to be seen in the best possible conditions. If the audience will be a small group, less than a dozen say, any good quality large-screen television set and VHS player with remote control will do. In addition:

- Make sure chairs are comfortable and arranged so that everyone has a clear view.

- Make sure there are no bright windows or lights behind the television, which would be distracting, or behind the audience, which would reflect in the television screen.

- Don't have total darkness for the showing, but leave on a soft low-level ambient lighting – people might want to take notes, and it's less strain on the eyes.

- If you can improve the sound by connecting up the audio outlet socket to a HiFi system and speakers, so much the better, as most television sets have fairly rudimentary sound systems.

- Check your show copy for any defects, such as drop out, from beginning to end, on the player you will be using.

- Double check that everything is ready, plugged in and working just beforehand.

Large groups

If your audience is more than a dozen, or constitutes a conference, then you will need to hire in special facilities, comprising one or more giant television screens and sound system. See the Useful Addresses section for a list of companies who offer this service in the United Kingdom – others can be found in the Production Manuals listed in the same section

Make sure there is adequate time for setting up and checking. You will also want to show your video on a higher quality format than simply a VHS distribution copy. The facilities company will provide Beta SP or high band U-matic players as appropriate.

Film

For small groups you can hire a 16mm film projector, screen and sound system. Have a projectionist with it so that you don't get involved in the machinery, and are free to address your audience. Have the room as dark as possible, since any stray light will significantly degrade the projected image.

For larger groups you can hire a small cinema known as a **preview theatre** (see Production Manuals under Useful Addresses for finding these facilities). These sometimes have catering facilities as well.

In both cases make sure you specify whether you are showing 16mm film or super 16mm film (see Chapter 7, Choosing a format).

ADVERTISING YOUR VIDEO

1. You should send free VHS copies of your video to any relevant trade or professional journals so that they can review it, in the same way that books are reviewed. You may even get some editorial copy offered if it is of special interest to their readers.

2. Send out brochures about your video to any company, institution or person you think would be interested. If you have a distributor they can do this for you, but you should still make sure they are mailing the right people.

MAKING FOREIGN VERSIONS

If your video turns out to be a huge success, you may be asked for copies to be shown in non-English speaking countries. In most cases all you will need to do is to have your commentary translated into the appropriate language, record it, and then go back to your music and effects sound track which you did at the on-line stage (see Chapter 8). You can then do a new on line, possibly incorporating foreign language titling as well, for considerably less money than your original on line, since the visuals will remain the same.

However, if foreign versions were not originally budgeted for, you will need to make sure you can recoup the extra costs with the foreign showings.

You may also need to do a standards conversion (see Chapter 7), depending on which country it is (see page 120), and to extend your music copyright clearance.

PACKAGING

If you have a distributor, they will handle this for you, but you may want to design the label on the cassette with reference to the subject or content of your video.

If you plan to distribute copies yourself, you will need to have labels printed, and to pack the cassettes for posting in suitably padded envelopes.

STORING YOUR MASTERS

Any tape, whether visual or audio, can be irreparably damaged by:

- heat
- violent shock
- any magnetic or electronic radiation
- damp.

In practice this means storing tapes in reasonably dry containers away from radiators, television sets, computers and other electronic devices. Even the electric motors on the London Underground can cause damage if tapes are too close to them.

If you are travelling by air, try to avoid having tapes put through the security scanning devices. They can easily be checked visibly by the security staff. This is particularly important with original camera tapes being sent or brought back from abroad.

Looking after film
Modern film emulsions withstand extremes of heat and cold surprisingly well. However, they are more likely to be affected if the storage temperature is continually changing than if it is kept more or less constant. You should also make sure your film is processed as soon as is practicable after exposure.

In practice the same precautions should be taken as with tape. A single X-ray dose from a properly adjusted airport security scanner should not cause problems, but it's better to be safe than sorry. Remember that if you freight your undeveloped film via air you have no real control over how many X-ray doses your material might receive. So whenever possible take it as hand luggage. Visual inspection is, of course, not possible as an alternative, since the film would be fogged.

Insuring your masters

Make sure that your original camcorder masters, or original negative in the case of film, as well as on-line masters, are covered by insurance against theft, fire, flood or other catastrophe. If you keep them in your own house, check that your Home Contents policy can include them. If not, then your production insurer (see Useful Addresses) should be able to arrange something. Some facilities companies may offer storage with insurance included, at an annual rate.

ENTERING FOR FESTIVALS

Winning an award, or even having a certificate of participation, always adds kudos to your video production. Usually your video will have to have been made after a certain date in order to qualify. Apart from the well-known cinema festivals, there are others which specialise in short films and videos, such as:

- **The British Short Film Festival** (September). *Address*: Room 313 BBC TV, Threshold House, 65–69 Shepherds Bush Green, London W12 7RJ. Tel: (0181) 743 8000, ext 62222/62052. Fax: (0181) 740 8540.

- **Edinburgh Fringe Film and Video Festival** (February). *Address:* 29 Albany Street, Edinburgh EH1 3QN. Tel: (0131) 556 2044. Fax: (0131) 557 4400.

- **Green Screen** (London's International Environmental Film Festival) (November). *Address*: 114 St Martin's Lane, London, WC2N 4AZ. Tel: (0171) 379 7390. Fax: (0171) 379 7197.

- **IVCA Awards For Effective Business Communication** (February). *Address*: International Visual Communications Associations, Bolsover House, 5–6 Clipstone Street, London W1P 7EB. Tel: (0171) 580 0962. Fax: (0171) 436 2606.

- **International Celtic Film and Television Festival** (March). *Address*: The Library, Farraline Park, Inverness IV1 1LS. Tel: (01463) 226 189. Fax: (01463) 716 368.

- **London Jewish Film Festival** (June). *Address*: National Film Theatre, South Bank, London SE1 8XT. Tel: (0171) 815 1322/1323. Fax: (0171) 633 0786.

- **Sheffield International Documentary Festival** (October). *Address*: The Workstation, 15 Paternoster Row, Sheffield S1 2BX. Tel: (0114) 276 5141. Fax: (0114) 2721849.

- **Video Positive** (April, odd years)). *Address*: International Biennale of Video and Electronic Media Art, Foundation for Art and Creative Technology, Bluecoat Chambers, Liverpool L1 3BX. Tel: (0151) 709 2663. Fax: (0151) 707 2150.

More festivals, both in the United Kingdom and elsewhere, are listed in the British Film Institute *Film and Television Handbook*, published annually (see Useful Addresses). There is usually a fee to enter a film or video, and a delegate's attendance fee, plus your travel and accommodation costs. If your project has been grant funded, you may be able to get your festival expenses covered as well. You may also be able to get yourself invited to the festival at the organiser's expense.

The British Council
Depending on the subject matter and intended audience of your video, it may be worth contacting the British Council, who maintain a list of festivals abroad, and who also themselves select films and videos to be shown at festivals and 'film weeks' overseas: *Address*: The British Council, Films Television and Video Department, 11 Portland Place, London W1N 4EJ. Tel: (0171) 389 3065. Fax: (0171) 389 3041.

Attending festivals
If your entry is chosen to participate (some are competitive, some are not), then it is well worth your while to attend if at all possible:

- to see what others in your field are doing

- to get more publicity for your video

- to make personal contact with possible distributors, and compare notes with other video-makers.

You will need to get in touch with the festival organisers well in advance. Before sending in any money make sure your video will fit into their field of interest.

Always remember that the real test of your video's success is how many of your targeted audience see it, and like it. Your video could still be doing a good job even if a festival audience is not impressed.

CHECKLIST

1. Make sure your first showing is easy to view, comfortable and hospitable.

2. Try to get feedback from your audience.

3. Send out brochures to journals and relevant institutions.

4. Make sure your masters are well stored and insured.

5. Look out for relevant festivals.

LOOKING TO THE FUTURE

Once you have completed your video and shown it, you can sit back and take stock of your situation. Whether you chose the DIY route and survived schizophrenia, or engaged volunteers or professionals, hopefully you will have found it a stimulating and rewarding experience, requiring interaction with others, and using problem-solving skills beyond the usual requirements of your occupation.

Be warned that you may well get bitten by the video/film-making bug, and want to move on to another project, making use of what you learned on the first one. Some of what you learned on the technical side may well be out of date, such is the speed of developments, even by the time your video is launched. But what you learned about getting it made, and about seeking out the most suitable technology for your project at an affordable cost, will be invaluable, regardless of future developments.

Finally, it's bound to be a very satisfying feeling if you have managed to reach your audience, whether or not you make any money out of it.

Further Reading

Basic Film Technique, Ken Daley (Focal Press Media Manual 1980).

Basics of Video Lighting, Des Lyver and Graham Swainson (Focal Press 1995).

Basics of Video Sound, Des Lyver (Focal Press 1995).

The Camcorder and Video Production Dictionary, Neil Everill (Pentland Press 1994).

Commissioning a Programme: The Professional Approach, IVCA (International Visual Communications Association 1988). See Useful Addresses.

The Complete Video Course: How to Make a Professional Home Video, Keith Brookes (Boxtree 1995).

Corporate and Instructional Video, Diane M. Gayeski (2nd edn, Prentice Hall).

Directing the Documentary, Michael Rabiger (2nd edn, Focal Press 1992).

Film and Video Budgets, Michael Wiese and Deke Simon (Focal Press 1995).

Film and Video Marketing, Michael Wiese (Focal Press 1989).

Film-Video Terms and Concepts, Steven E. Browne (Focal Press 1992).

Getting into Films & Television, Robert Angell (4th edn, How To Books 1997).

Grammar of the Edit, Roy Thompson (Focal Press–Media Manual 1993).

The Independent Film and Video Maker's Guide, Michael Wiese (Focal Press 1990).

The Low Budget Video Bible, Cliff Roth (2nd edn, New York: Desktop Video Systems 1995).

Music in Film and Video Productions, Dan Carlin Sr (Focal Press 1991).

Video Camera Techniques, Gerald Millerson (2nd edn, Focal Press 1994).

The Video Manual, David Cheshire (New York: Van Nostrand 1982).

Video Production Handbook, Gerald Millerson (2nd edn, Focal Press 1992).

The Video Production Organiser, Aleks Matza (Focal Press 1995).

Video Tape Editing: a Post-Production Primer, Steven E. Browne (2nd edn, Focal Press 1993).

Magazines for consumer video updates and articles, available in most high street newsagents, include:

Camcorder User (WV Publications and Exhibtions).

Video Camera (WV Publications and Exhibitions).

Useful Addresses

CAMERA FACILITIES

The Cruet Company Ltd, 11 Ferrier Street, London SW18 1SN. Tel: (0171) 874 2121.

Hammerhead Television Facilities Ltd, 42 Webbs Road, London SW11 6SF. Tel: (0171) 924 3977.

Orchid Video, The Old School House, Boston Manor, Bristol, Avon BS2 0RL. Tel: (0117) 941 3898.

Picture Canning Co Ltd, 3 Kimber Road, London SW18 4NR. Tel: (0181) 874 9277.

Stonehills Studios, Shields Road, Gateshead, Tyne and Wear NE10 0HW. Tel: (0191) 495 2244.

CONFERENCE FACILITIES

Conference Technical Facilities Ltd, Unit 6, Rufus Business Centre, Ravensburg Terrace, London SW18 4RL. Tel: (0181) 944 0300.

Mantascope Ltd, Douglas Drive, Godalming, Surrey GU7 1HJ. Tel: (01483) 419 894.

Market Factor, 6c West Treferton, Edinburgh EH7 6UL. Tel: (0131) 669 9899.

Medical Conference Organisers, Congress House, 65 West Drive, Cheam, Sutton SM2 7NB. Tel: (0181) 661 0877.

Quadrant Video Systems Ltd, 22 Lord Byron Square, Stowell Technical Park, Eccles New Road, Salford, Manchester M5 2XH. Tel: (0161) 745 9911.

DISTRIBUTORS

Boulton Hawker Films Ltd, Hadleigh, Ipswich, Suffolk IP7 5BG. Tel: (01473) 822 235.

Cinenova Promoting Films By Women, 113 Ronan Road, London E2 0HU. Tel: (0181) 981 6828.

Documedia International Films, Canada House, Blackburn Road, London NW6 1RZ. Tel: (0171) 625 6200.

Dangerous to Know, 66 Offley Road, London SW9 0LS. Tel: (0171) 793 9901. (Lesbian and gay.)

Duke Video, Milbourne House, St George's Street, Douglas, Isle of Man IM99 1PP. Tel: (01624) 623 634. (Motor sports.)

Masterclass Video Cassettes, 18 School Lane, Heaton Chapel, Stockport, Cheshire SK4 5DG. Tel: (0166) 376 410. ('How to' subjects.)

Medusa Communications, Regal Chambers, 51 Bancroft, Hitchin, Herts SG5 1LL. Tel: (01462) 421 818. (Various subjects.)

Pickwick Video, The Waterfront, Elstree Road, Elstree, Herts WD6 3BS. Tel: (0181) 207 6207. (Children and special interest.)

Visionary Communications Ltd, 28–30 The Square, St Annes-on-Sea, Lancs FY8 1RF. Tel: (01253) 712 453. (Various subjects.)

DUPLICATION AND CONVERSION

Audio Visual (London) Ltd, 3a Oakwood Business Park, Standard Road, London NW10 6EX. Tel: (0181) 961 9500.

Aztec Video Ltd, 7 Charlotte Mews, London W1P 1LN. Tel: (0171) 580 1591.

Duplication Express Ltd, Unit 9, City Business Park, Easton Road, Bristol BS5 0SP. Tel: (0117) 955 5599.

Humphries Video Services Ltd, Unit 2, The Willow Business Centre, 17 Willow Lane, Mitcham, Surrey CR4 4NX. Tel: (0181) 648 6111.

Masterclass Video Cassettes, 18 School Lane, Heaton Chapel, Stockport, Cheshire SK4 5DG. Tel: (0166) 376 3410.

Metropolis Duplication, 13 Shorts Gardens, Covent Garden, London WC2H 9AT. Tel: (0171) 240 9204.

Picardy Television, no. 1 Park Circus, Glasgow G3 7PB. Tel: (0141) 248 2070.

EDITING FACILITIES

Alan Afriat Associates, 24 Combemartin Road, London SW18 5PR. Tel: (0181) 789 2663.

Dateline Productions Ltd, 79 Dean Street, London W1V 5HA. Tel: (0171) 437 4510.

Digital Facilities Ltd, St George's Studios, 93–97 St George's Road, Glasgow G3 6JA. Tel: (0141) 333 9900.

Silverglade, 11a Enterprise House, 59–65 Upper Ground, London

SE1 9PQ. Tel: (0171) 827 9510.

Sync Facilities Ltd, The Media Centre, Station Road, Guiseley Leeds LS20 8EY. Tel: (01943) 877 323.

Workhouse Ltd, Granville House, St Peter Street, Winchester, Hampshire SO 23 8BP. Tel: (01962) 863 449.

FILM LABORATORIES

Filmatic Laboratories, 16 Colville Road, London W11 2BS. Tel: (0171) 221 6081.

Metrocolor London, 91–95 Gillespie Road, London N5 1LS. Tel: (0171) 226 4422.

Rank Film Laboratories Group, North Orbital Road, Denham, Uxbridge, Middx UB9 5HQ. Tel: (01895) 832 323.

Soho Images, 8–14 Meard Street, London W1V 3HR. Tel: (0171) 437 0831.

Technicolor, Bath Road, West Drayton, Middx UB7 0DB. Tel: (0181) 759 5432.

FILM STOCK

Kodak Ltd, Motion Picture and Television Imaging, PO Box 66, Station Road, Hemel Hempstead, Herts HP1 1JU. Tel: (01442) 61122.

Fuji Photo Film (UK), Cresta House, 125 Finchley Road, London NW3 6JH. Tel: (0171) 586 5900.

The Film Stock Centre, 68 Wardour Street, London W1V 3HP. Tel: (0171) 494 2244.

INSURANCE

Brian Hogg Group, Digby House, Causton Road, Colchester, Essex CO1 1YS. Tel: (01206) 577 612.

Robertson Taylor Insurance Brokers Ltd, 33 Harbour Exchange Square, London E14 9GG. Tel: (0171) 538 9840.

Sampson and Allen, One Kingly Street, London W1R 5LF. Tel: (0171) 287 5054.

MUSIC LIBRARIES

Applestone Music, 197 Union Street, Torquay, Devon TQ1 4BY. Tel: (01803) 292 050.

British Music Information Centre, 10 Stratford Place, London W1N
9AE. Tel: (0171) 499 8567.

De Wolfe Music Ltd, 80–88 Wardour Street, London W1V 3LF. Tel:
(0171) 439 8481.

Instamusic Ltd, 13 Rotherfield Avenue, Wokingham, Berkshire RG11
1EY. Tel: (01734) 782 408.

Jammy Music Publishers Ltd, The Beeches, 244 Anniesland Road,
Glasgow G13 1XA. Tel: (0141) 954 1873.

Magmasters, 20 St Anne's Court, Soho, London W1V 3AW. Tel: (0171)
734 0323.

Mediatracks, 93 Columbia Way, Blackburn, Lancashire BB2 7EA. Tel:
(01254) 691 197.

Sonoton Recorded Music Library, Fruit Farm House, Foxton, Cambs
CB2 6RT. Tel: (01763) 208 610.

PRODUCTION COMPANIES

Literally hundreds listed in the various production manuals – see
below.

PRODUCTION MANUALS

(Can be bought at a price, otherwise beg or borrow.)

The A to Z of Presenters, 123 Corporation Road, Gillingham, Kent
ME7 1RG. Tel: (01634) 851 077.

BFI Film and Television Handbook, The British Film Institute, 21
Stephen Street, London W1P 2LN. Tel: (0171) 255 1444.

Broadcast Production Guide, EMAP Business Communications Ltd,
33–39 Bowling Green Lane, London EC1R 0DA. Tel: (0171) 837
1212.

Kays Production Manual (Video Film and TV), Kays Publishing
Company, Pinewood Studios, Pinewood Road, Iver Heath, Bucks
SL0 0NH. Tel: (01753) 651 171.

Kemps Film TV and Video Handbook, Reed Information Services,
Windsor Court, East Grinstead House, East Grinstead, West
Sussex RH19 1XA. Tel: (01342) 326 972.

The Spotlight (actors and actresses), Spotlight Casting Directory and
Contacts, 7 Leicester Place, London WC2H 7BP. Tel: (0171) 437
7631.

The White Book, Birdhurst Ltd, Studio 27, Shepperton Studios,
Shepperton, Middlesex TW17 0QD. Tel: (01932) 572 622.

TRADE ASSOCIATIONS

Association of Professional Composers, 34 Hanway Street, London
W1P 9DE. Tel: (0171) 436 0919.
BAFTA (British Academy of Film and Television Arts), 195
Piccadilly, London W1V 9LG. Tel: (0171) 734 0022.
The British Council, Films Television and Video Department, 11
Portland Place, London W1N 4EJ. Tel: (0171) 389 3065.
BECTU (Broadcasting Entertainment Cinematograph and Theatre
Union), 111 Wardour Street, London W1V 4AY. Tel: (0171) 437
8506.
BKSTS (British Kinematograph Sound and Television Society),
M6–14 Victoria House, Vernon Place, London WC1B 4DF. Tel:
(0171) 242 8400.
IVCA (International Visual Communications Association), Bolsover
House, 5–6 Clipstone Street, London W1P 8LD. Tel: (0171) 580
0962.
PACT (Producers Alliance for Cinema and Television), Gordon
House, Greencoat Place, London SW1P 1PH. Tel: (0171) 233 6000.

WORKSHOPS

(Often distributors as well.)

A19 Film and Video, 21 Foyle Street, Sunderland SR1 1LE. Tel: (0191)
565 5709.
Black Audio Film Collective, 7–12 Greenland Street, London NW1
0ND. Tel: (0171) 267 0845/6.
City Eye, 1st Floor, Northam Centre, Kent Street, Notham,
Southampton SO1 1SP. Tel: (01703) 634 177.
Cornwall Video Resource, Royal Circus Buildings, Back Lane West,
Redruth, Cornwall TR15 2BT. Tel: (01209) 218 288.
Edinburgh Film Workshop Trust, 29 Albany Street, Edinburgh EH1
3QN. Tel: (0131) 557 5242.
Film Work Group, Top Floor, Chelsea Reach, 79–89 Lots Road,
London SW10 0RN. Tel: (0171) 352 0538.
Glasgow Film and Video Workshop, 3rd Floor, 34 Albion Street,
Merchant City, Glasgow G1 1LH. Tel: (0141) 553 2620.
Four Corners Film Workshop, 113 Roman Road, London E2 0QN.
Tel: (0181) 981 6111.
Lighthouse Film and Video, Brighton Media Production Centre, 11
Jew Street, Brighton BN1 1UT. Tel: (01273) 202 044.

London Electronic Arts, 3rd Floor, 5–7 Buck Street, London NW1 8NJ. Tel: (0171) 284 4588.

London Fields Film and Video, 10 Martello Street, London E8 3PE. Tel: (0171) 241 2997.

London Film Makers' Co-op, 12–18 Hoxton Street, London N1 6NG. Tel: (0171) 739 7117.

Media Arts, Town Hall Studios, Regent Circus, Swindon SN1 1QF. Tel: (01793) 493 451.

The Media Workshop, Peterborough Arts Centre, Media Department, Orton Goldhay, Peterborough PE2 0JQ. Tel: (01733) 237 073.

Mersey Film and Video, Bluecoat Chambers, School Lane, Liverpool L1 3BX. Tel: (0151) 708 5259.

Panico Workshop, 1 Falconberg Court, London W1V 5FG. Tel: (0171) 734 5120.

Sheffield Independent Film, 5 Brown Street, Sheffield S1 2BS. Tel: (0114) 272 0304.

Valley and Vale Community Arts, Blaengarw Workmen's Hall, Blaengarw, Nr Bridgend, Mid Glamorgan CF32 8AW. Tel: (01656) 871 911.

Vera Productions, 30–38 Dock Street, Leeds LS10 1JF. Tel: (0113) 242 8646.

WFA, Media and Cultural Centre, 9 Lucy Street, Manchester M15 4BX. Tel: (0161) 848 9785.

Western Eye Television, Easton Business Centre, Felix Road, Bristol BS5 0HE. Tel: (0117) 941 5854.

NOTE: These lists are by no means exhaustive. See *BFI Handbook* and production manuals for more.

World Video Standards

Algeria	PAL	Malaysia	PAL
Argentina	PAL	Malta	PAL
Australia	PAL	Mexico	NTSC
Austria	PAL	Morocco	SECAM
Bahamas	NTSC	Netherlands	PAL
Bahrain	PAL	New Zealand	PAL
Belgium	PAL	Nigeria	PAL
Belize	NTSC	Norway	PAL
Bermuda	NTSC	Philippines	NTSC
Brazil	PAL	Poland	PAL
Bulgaria	PAL	Portugal	PAL
Burma	NTSC	Romania	PAL
Canada	NTSC	Saudi Arabia	SECAM
Chile	NTSC	Singapore	PAL
China	PAL	South Africa	PAL
Cuba	NTSC	Spain	PAL
Czechoslovakia	PAL	Sweden	PAL
Denmark	PAL	Switzerland	PAL
Egypt	PAL	Syria	PAL/SECAM
Finland	PAL	Taiwan	NTSC
France	SECAM	Tanzania	PAL
Germany	PAL	Trinidad and	
Gibraltar	PAL	Tobago	NTSC
Hong Kong	PAL	Turkey	PAL
Hungary	PAL	United Arab	
India	PAL	Emirates	PAL
Iran	SECAM	United Kingdom	PAL
Iraq	SECAM	USA	NTSC
Ireland	PAL	USSR (former)	PAL
Israel	PAL	Yugoslavia	PAL
Jamaica	NTSC		
Japan	NTSC		
Jordan	PAL		
Luxembourg	PAL		

NOTE: Most former Eastern Bloc countries which used to be SECAM are now PAL.

Glossary

Analogue. Describes a process of recording or copying images and sound via another medium such as magnetic fields or film emulsion, most commonly on tape or film. Compare with **digital**.

Autocue. Device for enabling someone to read their lines while looking straight into the lens.

Beta SP. The tape format most commonly used for broadcast quality origination, and for making masters at the **on-line** stage from which distribution copies can be made.

Call sheet. A set of instructions giving all necessary logistical details for a day's shooting.

Camcorder. A video camera where the image capturing part, the 'camera', is combined with the tape recording mechanism to form one unit, instead of the older method of linking the two units with a cable.

Clapper board. A simple mechanical device with angled black and white stripes for easy visibility, used to identify and **synchronise** picture and sound when shooting film.

Colour temperature. A measurement of the colour of a light source in degrees Kelvin. The higher the temperature the bluer the light, e.g. daylight 5,000°K, tungsten light 3,200°K.

Commentary. A specially recorded voice layed over pictures and sound, which adds another dimension, complementing or filling out what the images say.

Contrast. The extent of the range of tones between the darkest and the brightest parts of an image. Stark sun and shadows is high contrast, a dull grey day is low contrast. The term applies both to the lighting, and to the tones in the subject itself.

Conversion. The process of copying a video tape recorded on one standard onto a new tape of another standard, e.g. **PAL** to **NTSC** or vice versa.

Cut. A point in the editing where one image or sound is juxtaposed directly with another. Also refers to editing stages, e.g. first cut, rough cut.

Cutting copy. See **workprint**.

Digital. Description of process of recording or copying images and sound, where constituents such as colour, light and dark, pitch, and so on, are broken down into electronic units, capable of being stored, reassembled, or manipulated electronically. Compare with **analogue**.

Dissolve. Editing term to describe the fading out of one image or sound superimposed on the fading in of the next image or sound.

Dolly. Any device on wheels for moving the camera during a shot. See **tracking**.

Drop-out. White blobs or lines seen on playing a videotape, caused by damage to, or imperfections in, the magnetic coating.

Dubbing. The mixing of different sound tracks in the final editing stage. Also the term for re-voicing dialogue in another language.

Duplication. The process of making copies from a master tape.

DV. The new digital video tape format for the consumer market.

EDL (edit decision list). A record of all the cuts and edits made **off line**, usually expressed in **time code** numbers.

Fogging. Degradation of the blacks and shadows in an image caused by unwanted exposure to light, or to X-ray radiation.

Format. The type, shape and size of a recording medium, either tape or film or disk.

Frame. One complete television picture in video, or a single image on a length of film.

Grip. Crew member responsible for operating tracking and craning devices.

HI-8. Small, long playing, high resolution tape format used in domestic camcorders, and increasingly for broadcast programmes. Likely to be superseded by DV.

Iris. Adjustable opening in a lens to control the amount of light allowed through, thus controlling exposure of the image.

Key numbers. Numbers, or barcodes, put on the edge of film stock during manufacture which print through to the **workprint**, allowing frame-accurate matching of negative to workprint when finally cutting the negative.

Linear. A term to describe a method of editing where any cut involves a copy, and any alterations mean recopying from that point, or redoing the edits. Compare with **non-linear**.

Magic hour. The time between sunset and darkness when there is still enough skylight to take pictures.

Mixed lighting. Lighting where light sources of differing colour temperatures illuminate the scene, e.g. daylight and electric light in a room.

Monitor. A television set which will accept a video input signal, from a camcorder, for checking pictures while shooting. Can become rather like a school prefect!

Montage. A sequence of shots cut together so as to build up an overall impression, without continuity of action.

Narration. A specially recorded voice layed over pictures to help tell a story, or to complement the pictures. Often used in the same sense as **commentary**.

Neg cutting. The process of cutting an original film negative to match the final edit of the workprint.

Non-linear. A term to describe a system of editing where you can flit about and make alterations wherever you want, without the necessity of recopying or starting again. Compare with **linear**.

NTSC (National Television Standards Committee). The video standard which is used for origination and transmission in the United States of America and certain other countries.

Off line. A term used to describe the trial and error editing which takes place on a cheap and convenient tape format, before making the final master edit from the original material.

On line. A term used to describe the process where the edit decisions arrived at during the **off-line** stage (see above) are finally implemented to create the new edited master.

PAL (Phase Alternate Line). The video standard which is used for origination and transmission in the United Kingdom and many other countries.

Paper edit. A system of cutting up typed transcripts of interviews and pasting together selected sections in the desired order.

Playback. Viewing a recorded video image to check whether it is satisfactory. Also used to refer to the playing of a prerecorded music track in order to shoot images in **synchronisation** with it.

Release forms. A document signed by interviewees or other participants, allowing their contribution to be used in specified circumstances.

Resolution. The ability of a lens and recording system, either tape or film, to record fine detail. There are various ways of measuring resolution, e.g. number of lines, per millimetre, which can be distinguished as separate lines.

Rough cut. The editing stage where the main decisions have been made about stucture, but polishing and fine tuning have yet to be done.

Rubber numbers. A set of numbers, usually based on scene or slate numbers, printed at regular intervals along the edges of a film workprint and magnetic sound track. They are used during the editing stage to maintain **synchronisation** when sections have been cut up into short lengths, and for identification. They do not relate to the original negative. Compare with **time code**.

Rushes. The result of a day's shooting, or the film print received back from the laboratory the next day. (Known as 'dailies' in the USA.)

SECAM (Sequential Colour and Memory). A system of colour television transmission used in France and certain other countries.

Shooting script. The script used during shooting which lays out details of visuals and audio, for the benefit of everyone involved in the shooting.

Slate number. Used to sequentially number the shots during shooting. Not the same as 'scene number', which is allocated in the script.

Standards. A term referring to technical specifications involving colour coding, frames per second and number of 'lines' in the picture, as well as other details. **PAL** and **NTSC** are the two current standards, and they are incompatible.

Steenbeck. A machine for viewing a reel of film, with one or more sound tracks, which has fast forward, rewind and slow motion functions.

S-VHS. Tape format similar to **VHS**, but yielding better quality picture and sound. The improvement factor in it is not compatible with VHS.

Synchronisation. The process of ensuring that picture and sound, and additional cameras if necessary, run at exactly the same speed over the duration of a shot. Also refers to the reconstitution of matching picture and sound by means of **time code, clapper boards** and **rubber numbers** during the editing stage.

Talking head. Term used to describe a head and shoulder shot of a person speaking in an interview, or statement to camera. Often used derogatively, e.g. 'The programme was nothing but talking heads'.

Telecine. A device for scanning a filmed image in order to turn it into a video signal, either for transfer to tape, or for transmission.

Time code. An electronic system of numbering each frame of video or film, for logging purposes, for **synchronisation**, and for retrieval of material by any compatible editing machinery. It can be initiated during shooting, or at the beginning of editing.

Tracking. A movement through space of the camera during the shot in a horizontal direction.

Track laying – 1. The editing process of fitting various sound tracks to the picture, which will later be mixed to form one track.

Track laying – 2. The laying down of special rails for a **dolly** to travel along in a tracking shot.

Treatment. A document setting out the main aims and intentions of a project, and outlining the ground to be covered.

VCR (video cassette recorder). A device for recording a video signal, either from a television transmission or direct from a video camera. It is also used to play back through a monitor or television set.

VHS. The tape format used in most domestic VCRs, and in the first generation of camcorders.

Vignetting. Term to describe the effect of a soft-edged, circular mask around the image. Caused by using a lens of insufficient covering power, or by a constricting lens hood. Can also be a deliberate effect.

Vox pops. Short interviews with passers-by, usually in the street, to get opinions on a topic. From the Latin *vox populi* – voice of the people.

White balance. A means of adjusting the colour signals from a video camera so that something which is pure white will be recorded as pure white, without a colour cast. It may be automatic or manual.

Workprint. The film print from an original negative, which is used for cutting up and editing.

Index

125